VOICES FROM THE INAUDIBLE

Ritual (with a preface by Sigmund Freud)
The Unknown Murderer
Surprise and the Psychoanalyst
From Thirty Years with Freud
Masochism in Modern Man
A Psychologist Looks at Love
Psychology of Sex Relations
Dogma and Compulsion
Listening with the Third Ear
Fragment of a Great Confession
The Secret Self
The Haunting Melody
The Search Within
Of Love and Lust
Sex in Man and Woman
Myth and Guilt
Mystery on the Mountain
The Creation of Woman
The Temptation
Jewish Wit
The Need to be Loved
Pagan Rites in Judaism

· Farrar, Straus and Company · New York

VOICES FROM THE INAUDIBLE

The patients speak

THEODOR REIK

Contents

I This book

1 About the middle of May

Some shattering noise coming through the open window—
perhaps that of a car collision—woke me from my afternoon nap. It is strange that I now need a short sleep during the day and that I am still tired. Still the repercussions
of the heart attack I had many months ago?

It is only the middle of May, 1963, and it is already so
warm. Well, only a few weeks more and I shall go to the
mountains. And then no psychoanalytic patients any longer;
only consultations in which I will refer patients to my most
reliable and experienced students, and a few supervision
or control sessions for young psychoanalysts. Just enough
to make a modest living. My God, I have passed seventy-
five and I am entitled to a kind of semiretirement during
which I would like to write some more books. This has always been my real ambition. I was never a fanatic therapist; as a matter of sober fact I was mediocre in this area,
but I was eager to find some hidden truths. Yes, the books
I wrote are the best of me. I can write, but one pays for
each ability by some other incompetence. I cannot even
turn the radio on properly.

While I stretch myself out on the couch, the memory of
the birthday celebration that my organization, my friends,
and students gave me at the St. Regis Hotel is suddenly
revived; the splendid hall, many hundreds of people. I was

flooded with congratulations and wishes of many happy returns of the day. I was standing there between my two daughters when many young women friends, students, and even some unknown ladies came over to kiss me. My younger daughter Miriam smiled sweetly when another woman asked me "May I kiss you?" but the older one, Irene, whispered: "The ladies are beginning to get formal."

Then there were the speeches of prominent psychoanalysts, of the doctors Eidelberg, Sandor Lorand, and Sandor Rado. Each of those colleagues and friends found something to praise in my writings and in my personality and expressed some original ideas about them. One, for instance, pointed out that the "self-revelation" contained in my books proved my moral courage.

I felt happy and humble at the same time. It flashed through my mind that in a similar situation Freud had once said that he could defend himself when attacked but was entirely defenseless when praised. (I don't remember any longer whether he added Hamlet's line "I am poor even in thanks.")

Then came the reading of the many telegrams and congratulatory letters from psychoanalytic and psychological associations and from individuals, among them Mr. and Mrs. John F. Kennedy. That was only two weeks ago. I hope I have thanked everybody who wrote or sent a telegram.

Urged by all to say a few sentences I rose, embarrassed, and did not know what I would say. The reference to my "self-revelation" in one of the speeches helped me then. I confessed that I had been very discouraged when I landed here as a poor refugee from the Nazis in June 1938. I was then past fifty, had few friends in the States—what was to become of me?

But soon my courage returned. I began to work and to write again and I soon had a few neurotic patients for psychoanalysis. The next years were filled with work and with the worry of providing enough for my wife, who was ill, and my children. (The heart attack occurred shortly after my wife's death.)

And now? I certainly could have kept my promises better and kept more of them, but I had done my best. There are not many miles any longer before I sleep. I have finished with the deeply felt but badly expressed thanks to all. That was only two weeks ago. And now I feel grateful to a quite different kind of people.

2 Thinking of patients

Saying good-by to regular psychoanalytic practice and to patients, I suddenly become aware how many psychological insights I owed to them, how much they had extended my horizon and deepened my understanding.

In the course of time they told me, little by little, their life stories and their case histories. But they also told me a lot of other things—things beyond the pathological and the pathetic, beyond the trite and the trivial.

My main interest was directed not to the therapy of neurotic disturbances but to the problems of general psychology and applied psychoanalysis. How much they helped me! Not only by their "self-revelations" but also by the thousands of wise and witty things they had said during those fifty-odd years of clinical psychoanalytic practice. Did I not collect those sayings—sometimes only clues —somewhere?

Abruptly I get up from the couch, no longer tired, and dismiss all daydreams and memories and walk over to my writing table. Folders full of such material must be in one of those compartments. Here, indeed, are bulky folders of those sayings. I open the folders and look through the abundance of notes, sometimes only a few words on a piece of paper.

But did I not already publish some of those sayings? Of

course, there was that young girl I treated here in the States, soon after I arrived. I admired her sentence "When I am shabbily dressed, I hate everybody."

Looking through this wealth of material I am again and again surprised by the precision and felicity of expressions in so many of those sentences, of their honesty and straightforwardness, often by their crude matter-of-factness. Many are, so to speak, communications "from the gut"—all wrappings removed, the truth as it is felt and thought, unvarnished and unembroidered.

Not all sayings take their origin from "emotion recollected in tranquillity." Some were uttered with all kinds of actually felt emotions, agitated, ironical, humorous, desperate, even in reflections on experiences and in reliving them. Looking through the papers I find, for instance, the clue *elderly lady.* The patient had first been in psychoanalytic treatment with a woman psychiatrist. When he came to me, he told me that he and she did not understand each other very well. He had once told her "You are an elderly lady and you can't dig me." That had, of course, been a very courteous circumlocution. What he really wanted to say was "You're an old bitch!" What a bliss it would have been really to say it in those very words! In other cases patients surprised themselves by what they had said in their analytic sessions—sometimes the most amusing and amazing things they conveyed without consciously thinking them out before.

This book does not pretend to be research in depth, but it will perhaps lead to such depth. It contributes a singular new territory to our psychological knowledge. In bringing this kind of spontaneous thought and impulse into the open, the patients added significant features to the image of man. It is not important that what is here noticed comes from neurotic patients. What is valuable is that these ut-

terances came from people "even as thou and I." Here are
precepts of human experience leading to sometimes pro-
fane and sometimes profound insights. We psychoanalysts
are holding up the mirror to the innermost thoughts and
feelings of human beings. But in this particular case we are
holding up the mirror in such a way that also the reader
can also see the faces and hear the voices.

I am still wondering why no other analyst has thought
that it would be helpful to collect those spontaneous expressions of thought and emotion. Here is mental life in
the raw, flung from the center. Yet I know that the more
important material is not what patients say, but what is
expressed in silence—in the pauses between their sentences. Here is the unsayable and sometimes the unspeaka-
ble.

3 Only voices remain

Often I do not remember the faces of the patients whose sentences I jotted down. I only remember their words and the tone and timbre of their voices. The French psychologists used to differentiate between a *type visuel* and a *type auditif*, people whose memories are more of a visual or an auditory kind. There are, of course, mixed types. (Freud was predominantly visual.)

It is strange too that I do not remember the names of the people I am quoting here. Here is a piece of paper with the initials *P. D.*, with some added words. For the life of me I don't remember who that was. What's in a name?

Yet Freud often admonished us, his Viennese circle of students, to pay attention to names because they have an important role in the life of patients. We should even ask for names, he said, and added that we unconsciously connect certain images or ideas with persons' names. If those names are not known, the image of the persons are blurred or indistinct in our minds. He compared such a notion to the *dramatis personae* in modern plays in which the characters are identified only as father, mother, sister, uncle, friend, a neighbor. They remain figures without a name and almost without a face.

My lamentable memory for names has, it now occurs to me, an advantage; it exercises a correct discretion. It is, of course, understood that the people whose sentences I quote here are anonymous, but in this particular case identification became impossible on account of my bad memory. . . . Discretion is the better part of valor.

I am sure that most of those patients will not themselves remember what they so casually said in psychoanalytic sessions many years ago. Yes, it is even possible that one or another of them might read the book in which he is quoted without recognizing himself. They appear here no longer as individuals but as voices. Only their voices remain. It is almost ghostly. . . .

In the projected book I would have to mark the sex, of course, to say who was a woman or a man, perhaps occasionally the age and the profession, sometimes adding that they are single or married.

The collection of sayings could become quite an informative and illustrative book: Moments of truths preserved. The last masks doffed. I think of Arthur Schnitzler's play *The Last Mask* and for an instant I see myself walking with the writer on the Sommerhaidenweg in Vienna. How long ago that was!

4 Another folder

I put that folder aside and take up another, bulkier one. I recognize its content. Notes and notices from seminars, psychoanalytic contributions of my students—with some from myself—perhaps containing some unexpected insights. Should I not include them in the projected book as an extra group?

Freud told us that emotions and thoughts that are not connected with words or word presentation remain unconscious. The most important emotions and thoughts we have to deal with in psychoanalysis originate in that twilight zone in which no words are yet born. We have to bring them to expression—sometimes with labor pains. What patients say often amounts to a breakthrough from this area. The most valuable things they express are not those which can easily be said.

And here? What my students said in their analytic sessions, in supervision analysis, and in seminars was also often worked out from that twilight zone to verbal expressions. I owe much to some of those gifted young people in the seminars.

Suddenly a memory from my childhood emerges. My brother Otto, fifteen years older (the Nazis killed him in Vienna), sometimes brought a young man home from his school. I knew him only as "Uncle Arnold" when I was a little boy. He was friendly enough toward me. Sometimes he sat down at the piano and played some wild tunes, quite different from the familiar melodies to which my ears were accustomed. Many years later I learned that he was Arnold Schönberg, perhaps the most prominent composer after Gustav Mahler.

I followed his life and knew about his later vicissitudes although I still did not understand some of his music. I knew that he fled from the Nazis to Paris, where he returned publicly in a symbolic gesture to the Judaism he had abandoned in 1921. He lived in Los Angeles at the time when I too already lived in the States. He died there in 1951.

How had the name of Arnold Schönberg entered my thoughts? Some years ago I came by chance upon his book *Harmonielehre* and opened it. The first sentence I read was in his foreword: "This book I have learned from my students." I could, of course, say the same for that part of my own projected book.

I still remember at least the general idea of some of the succeeding sentences from Schönberg's foreword. He says that the movement originates in the teacher and his unrest must be transferred to his students. Then they will be in search just as he is. That movement which originates in the teacher must return to him. In this sense, the composer says, he learned his book from his students and he has to thank them. Thus must I.

5 Parts

Thinking of this projected book I consider the possibilities of its parts, how to divide that amassed material into portions. The simplest thing would be a division of sayings into those of women and those of men. Women would come first; what they say about themselves, men, women friends, and so on. Ladies first, not merely on account of gallantry, but also because women are in general more articulate and have a lively and rich vocabulary. I anticipate that I shall find plenty of witty and malicious remarks by women in the folder. Do not all women agree in their views on men in certain directions? For instance that all men are impatient, even when they are watchmakers; that they are often so unreasonable (especially when those men don't understand feminine logic) and that they are all so transparent (especially in sexual matters). And men? They also agree in their general opinions about women: that they are perplexingly devious and utterly inscrutable, that they are unaccountably moody and change their minds—if minds they have at all—that they buy all they see in store windows. (A joke Freud once made flits through my mind: "Wives are expensive, but one has them for a long time.")

Such a division will perhaps simplify things too much. There are overlapping areas in which the sexual differentiation or variations are of no importance: general problems or questions of everyday life. Well, perhaps there could be a part entitled *Miscellany*.

The last part would be the collection of remarks and sayings from supervision psychoanalysis and seminars.

But all this has time. And what's so important about the parts of the book? I shall play it by the third ear when I am looking through that material—that material which is also part of the "talking cure," as Anna O, an early patient of Breuer and Freud, called psychoanalysis in 1895. Here are characteristic and unblushing utterances, intimate, powerful, and lively voiced. No conventional strings attached to them; as such they are valuable as moments of truth.

I push the folders back into the compartment. Lines from the *Prologue in the Theatre* from *Faust*, known by heart since my teens, run through my mind:

> *Lasst uns auch so ein Schauspiel geben!*
> *Greift nur hinein ins volle Menschenleben!*
> *Ein jeder lebt's, nicht vielen ist's bekannt,*
> *Und wo ihr's packt, da ist's interessant.*

> [Shift your scenes rapidly; write fast and gaily,
> Give, in your play, the life we witness daily.
> The life which all men live, but few men notice,
> Yet which will please ('tis very strange, but so 'tis)
> Will please, when forced again on their attention
> More than the wonder of remote invention.]

The middle of May and so warm! Only a few weeks more and I'll take all that material to the mountains with me. I'll sort it there, arrange it and begin to write the book.

II Women about women

1. Women are the most unsparing and penetrating critics of other women. In chattering they often make caustic and sarcastic remarks about dress and manners, the mental shortcomings and emotional moods of their acquaintances and even of their friends. This does not, of course, exclude their making a common front against a man or men when women are criticized or attacked.

Critical remarks, more or less poisonous, about other women are often exchanged among women friends. This also takes place in psychoanalytic situations which remove the conventional inhibitions and urge men and women to express their thoughts freely.

What follows is a collection of such impulsive, often indiscreet, and interesting remarks by some women about others.

2. One college girl about another: "She always foresees calamity and a bad outcome to everything and she expresses satisfaction when she is proven right. I wonder if Cassandra always said 'I told you so'?"

3. The same, after a conversation with a young man: "Men are so stupid. John talked about Anne yesterday. He really thinks she is a dangerous woman, a kind of *femme fatale*. He is afraid of her and calls her a witch. If he

would change the first letter of that word, he would characterize her more correctly."

Girl in her twenties about a girl friend: "The man in her life? I would rather use the plural than the singular. There are always several."

4. Middle-aged woman: "I am not a gossip, so help me God! I am gossiped to and I only repeat what I have heard from others."

5. One society woman about another: "She always says that she has no secrets. Her life is an open book. I wanted to add: 'A pornographic one.'"

About the same person: "She always says: 'On second thought I decide to do this or that.' I consider this a grotesque exaggeration because I don't believe that she even has a first thought."

On another occasion: "Her private life is as secret as that of a Hollywood star. She publicizes it." About another woman: "She is a witch, but her broomstick must always be in the latest fashion."

6. A woman about another one living across the street: "Every afternoon she has a date. She does not yet know, of course, with which man."

7. One patient discussing compliments: "There are compliments a woman pays to another; these can be compared to certain Indian poisons about which I read recently. At first they are almost not felt. They develop their fatal effect within the organism only after some time."

About another woman: "She has very sharp claws in her velvet gloves."

8. One patient at the beginning of the summer: "Yesterday I was in the solarium to get a good suntan. There were only much older women there. Their skin was as wrinkled and shriveled as that of an elephant."

9. Another malevolent criticism is based on the behavior of older women. A lady remarks about an older acquaintance: "She has a rich vicarious emotional life because she has many women friends whose troubles she enjoys. When she has no visitors, she looks at television, on which she also sees plenty of misery."

10. A college girl speaks about her aunt: "When you listen to her talking of our family for a longer time you get the impression that she has prepared premature obituaries in her thoughts for every relative."

11. A good insight into the relationship of girls of the same age is given by spontaneous declarations such as these: "I would not dream of asking Anne to go shopping with me for that dress. She knows I am going to this party where she is not invited. She is perhaps envious or mischievous or competitive. She would probably suggest a dress that would not be becoming to me at all."

"I told you about my roommate Anne. She is really a snake in the grass and life with her is not a paradise. Far from it. . . . Well, the day before yesterday when I came home from the office, a note from her was on my table. She had written *Please go to the movies after 9 o'clock.* I knew, of course, what this meant. Anne expected her boy friend and wanted to go to bed with him. Therefore she wished me out of the apartment. I could not help feeling envious although I would not do the same before my marriage. I saw Anne then in the morning before I left for the office. She did not say anything about her boy friend, but she looked satisfied and happy."

12. Woman after visiting a rich acquaintance: "After a visit she treated me with such icy politeness that I felt chilled." The same: "She would never call a spade a spade, but would perhaps allude to it as to an agricultural tool."

About another, an obese woman: "Do you know that Nancy is falling in love with that man? You should see Nancy in love. It's funny. The fat is in the fire."

13. Malicious remarks such as those quoted do, however, not exclude the occasional emergence of friendly feelings toward other women: "Debbie has beautiful legs and she wears dresses reaching to her ankles. It means a kind of self-sabotage and I told her she renounces thereby her chances with men.

"We had a furious quarrel. When I left her, I caught myself wishing she should have psoriasis on her face and arms. You know I often envied her complexion. It is like a peach."

14. About a society figure: "That woman is such a hard and energetic climber that she will finally arrive at the top —except, of course, should she have an unexpected accident and suddenly be precipitated from a great height. She passionately endeavors to live up to the image of an elegant society lady that she has made of herself. She had only three or four great passions in her life. Her casual affairs could, of course, not be counted any longer."

15. "When I moved out of the apartment, I asked Anne whether I could take some records with me and she said 'Yes.' I then forgot about them and when I asked her again, she said 'But Debby'—that's her new roommate—'likes them and often plays them.' After a few weeks I visited her and wanted to take at least a few records home. She was in a foul mood and threw things at her cat. The animal was very frightened. I thought, she treats me exactly as she does her cat. When I asked her to leave the animal alone she said 'Oh, that does not matter. The cat knows I love her.'"

About another woman: "She is very big, like a ship with

flapping sails. She hopes that she will enter a harbor some-where. As far as I can see she navigates without steering."

16. Young girl: "I think women are incomplete beings. They need a man and perhaps even a child in order not to feel alone."

17. A woman about a girl who is still single: "She said to me 'It's so sweet of you to be so sweet to me.' She is such an oily hypocrite. Later on we discussed her chances and I told her 'But why do you worry, honey? You will marry a rich man. If you retain your fine taste for luxury, he will, of course, become a beggar after a few years, but that's another story.' I hope I ruined her day with that remark; at all events I made mine."

"I always say 'Speak the truth and shame the devil.' The only trouble is, the devil cannot be put to shame." Later on: "She took me up to her first-floor apartment and showed me all her dresses and furs. It was as if she counted her blessings right in front of me. . . . She is not satisfied to keep up with the Joneses; she has to surpass them."

18. After she had spent an evening with another woman, the patient reports: "She talked and talked and talked until I felt as if I had been brainwashed—with a perfumed soap, too. She is never bored when she can talk. Only when others are talking is she weary."

19. A college girl about another: "I ran into Jane and told her that I would go to Radcliffe and she told me that she was accepted at Bennington. I asked her 'Isn't that that finishing school in Vermont?' "

20. Middle-aged woman imagining another woman in a strange part: "If she were acting Hamlet, she would say 'To be loved or not to be loved'—that is the question she asks herself whenever she meets an eligible man." The

same woman on another occasion: "She believes that God made the seasons of the year to give her occasions to buy new dresses."

21. Girl in her middle twenties working toward a Ph.D. in anthropology: "The women of Central Australia and New Guinea were not in such a subjugated position as the early explorers and missionaries describe. . . . They did at least not worry about what they should wear on certain occasions."

22. After an evening of bridge: "That woman has only one passion—bridge. At the bridge table she is full of temperament. I cannot imagine that she is otherwise sensitive and I do not believe she is temperamental in bed, neither with her husband nor with any other man."

About a society woman: "She has a cook, a maid, and a butler and she spends a great deal of her time lying on the couch because she says she is so nervous. Yes, she is most of her time on the couch, either alone or with a man—in a kind of group therapy, you might call it."

23. "She is a natural joiner, but she has no idea whom or what she is joining. She once told me that she never knows what she will say at those meetings until she hears herself saying it. Well, perhaps then the others don't know what she is saying."

24. Middle-aged woman about a young married couple: "I ran into the husband and we chatted a while, also about his wife. He said he considered himself a lucky dog because he got her. He should have called her a bitch who ran after him until he married her." Later about the same woman: "It is easy enough to put her in her place, but it is almost impossible to keep her there."

About another woman: "Her husband did not want any children. He lived only for his work, the real-estate business. She was faithful to him and only recently—after almost twenty years of married life—she began an affair with a journalist whose worthlessness she clearly recognizes. But she says that he is in love with her. After some months she told her husband all about the affair. I still don't understand why she did this. Perhaps she wanted to show her husband that she is still desirable to other men. Or did she want to punish him? He is almost never affectionate with her. By the way, he did not make much ado about her affair. He treats it as if it were not very important."

On another occasion: "I hate to have another woman in the kitchen except helping me washing the dishes."

25. Critical female dance teacher to her class: "When you make the turn, take your left breast with you." To a student: "From your waist up you're a butterfly, but from the waist down you're a goat."

26. Life with sister. A young girl complains: "My younger sister is a pest and provokes everybody in the family. I often feel that I should give her a good crack because she wishes to control all of us."

27. Uncertainty of a young girl: "I never know whether I am overdressed or underdressed for a party before I see the other people there. It is as with a steak. You don't know whether it is just right for a person until you see him eat it."

"I was myself surprised by the success of my lying. I was almost proud of it, as if I had discovered in myself a talent for some artistic creation."

28. Woman psychiatrist: "You often hear men assert that women have no morals; they mean, of course, ethics in the sense of Kant, of a code of morality. But in reality women have morals of their own, quite different from the system of men, perhaps deeply rooted in women's biological functions."

29. Nineteen-year-old college girl: "My mother always said, 'I sacrificed myself for you; all my life I always took care of you alone.' She tortured me to death with her self-sacrifice."

30. The mother of this girl in a consultation with me: "I don't know whether it is only a *façon de parler* of the young generation or if it is serious. My daughter was having lunch yesterday at home and she soon rushed away. I asked her why she was hurrying so much and where she had to go. You know what she said? 'I have to get laid.' "

31. About a younger woman: "She treats her chastity as she treats her summer dresses. When they occasionally get dirty she obeys the principle 'Wash and wear them.' "

32. Woman about her teen-aged daughter: "My husband asked me: 'Is Jeanne still on the telephone?' and I answered 'She has not yet been off it today.' "

33. About a woman friend: "There was a buffet supper and Emily went four times to refill her plate. I was pleased because she is beginning to get obese, and when she eats so much she will be fat in a short time. I whispered to her, of course, 'Watch your figure!' but I knew it was in vain."

About the scene before that party: "My friend Anne came in just when I was dressing to go out. I asked her 'How do you like my new dress?' 'I like it,' she said, 'but it's so dressy.' Now, I ask you: What else should an evening dress be than dressy?"

About a certain woman: "She is always busy pouring oil on untroubled water."

"I hate to be one of the first guests at a party, so I took my time in dressing and making up and I really got there when some of the other guests were already leaving."

About her friend Anne: "At the party a very rich man who has an estate on Fire Island was discussed. Someone said that that man is a snob and his mansion is a meeting

place of many fairies during the summer month
way back in my car Anne asked me why the go
assembled at that place on Fire Island. She had
what *fairies* mean in New York language."

About a young girl: "She is semifancy-free an
engaged. You don't understand this? I mean she sa
two things—of course, to different men."

34. Young woman: "I look so awful today that
dare to look into a mirror." Another woman about th
"During the twenty years I have known her, her ha
had all the colors you could imagine—except its n
color, of course."

35. Woman telling the story of her life: "My room
in college gave me the first real instruction about sex.
was not only experienced herself, but she was explicit
showed me the facts of sexual life in pantomime."

36. Society woman about her activities the preced
day: "I went from one fitting to another and then to t
committee meeting of my club; from there I had to go to
fashion show and then I had to rush home to dress for th
dinner to which I had invited ten people. Entertainin
exhausts me."

37. Woman about herself: "I am a compulsive liar.
often lie when it is not necessary at all, but I do not know
why. I cannot say everything I would like to and must keep
a lot of things to myself."

38. Describing the entrance of a woman at a party:
"Then she came in covered with a black evening dress,
with a lot of costume jewelry and with mascara."

39. "People say flattery is only skin-deep. Yet I like
compliments paid to me. I think my skin is responsive to
them."

40. "She said: 'It's beneath my dignity to answer,' but I
do not believe in the dignity of women. They only give

themselves airs. They are all women and they know it."

41. An actress, accompanying her description with pantomime: "People talk a lot of hot air about the charm of
Viennese women. Such a female enters a room, for instance
at a party, goes straight forward to a chair and sits down
like that, you see? Should I show you how we were taught
to sit down? We walk to the chair and then make one
step backward in order to sit down. Is this not more
graceful?"

42. About a society woman who arranges dinners and
dances for philanthropic causes: "It is easy for her to win
friends and influence people, but then it is difficult for
them to get rid of her."

43. From the conversation of two middle-aged women
who both came to the United States from Vienna after
Hitler occupied the city: "Please, Erica, don't make a fuss
about the affair your husband is having and don't threaten
to divorce him. Believe me, if all wives whose husbands
have affairs left them, we would have only divorced women
in this country. You threatened to divorce him four years
ago when you found out about him and that actress and
yet you stayed with him, and you will stay with him now
too. Do you remember what they said in Vienna: 'Nothing
is eaten as hot as it was cooked.' "

44. "Her dresses are always tastefully chosen; she is always well combed and tries to make the best impression.
What a pity she is not attractive!"

45. Woman telling her life story: "When I was fourteen
years old, my mother became pregnant and my brother
was born. I was so ashamed before the girls in school. My
mother was too old for sex."

46. "I asked her what she would wear at her divorce
hearing and told her that I thought her heavy crêpe blouse
and a long crêpe skirt would be quite suitable."

47. "She really lost weight quickly. Either she fell in love or she has found a very efficient diet."

48. "She wanted to marry a man with whom she could be as bitchy as she really is."

49. "She wore pants. You know, the kind they now call toreador pants. That brought Spanish bullfighters to mind. But then I thought, she is only a cow."

50. "She showed me the gymnastic exercises she does in the morning to keep herself fit. But I suspect she performs them as a rehearsal so she can cross her legs over a man's back at night."

51. Girl: "I want to go to Lord and Taylor and I must dress very carefully. The salesgirls study you very attentively and don't show you certain dresses when you are not dressed well."

52. Substitute teacher: "It is funny; the less money I have, the more I spend on clothes and nylon stockings. I must not neglect my appearance. The other women teachers observe how I am dressed."

53. About a society woman: "She is a lion-huntress and she serves her prey at the little dinner parties she gives."

54. "A man will sometimes look at another man, but a woman will always look another woman over."

55. Middle-aged woman: "A woman sometimes has secrets from herself. It is as if she puts away a thing of which she is ashamed into a certain hiding place and forgets it from then on."

The same woman, in another psychoanalytic session: "Women often don't pay much attention to the actual words men say to them, but more to the undertones, and thus develop a strong instinct for articulate signals."

56. College girl who is studying English literature: "When I was ill, I read a lot of poetry while I was lying in bed. I had high temperature and for a day or two I was

afraid that I would die. I was then haunted by the lines of a poem by Andrew Marvell. Don't you know it:

> 'The grave's a fine and private place,
> But none, I think, do there embrace.'?

I thought then how stupid I had been not to give in to Jack—you know, the boy who asked me so often to come to his room."

57. A worldly wise woman: "There are few women who never asked themselves on certain occasions 'How easy or how hard should a woman make it for a man?' I think no man is troubled with questions of such a kind. He perhaps asks himself only 'When will she give in?' "

58. A college girl: "We had a few drinks and went up to his room. You guess what happened there. Well, I have not much character, you know."

59. Woman about a man: "He was very passionate when he approached me sexually. You heard it in his breathing, but during his lovemaking he often got out of breath—also in a sexual direction." The same woman about another man: "We talked about a hundred different subjects in order to avoid talking about our relationship."

"I have had that maid since I married and she knew all about my affair. She always opened the door to my lover when he came in in the afternoon. She became the willing accomplice of my adultery."

60. Very old lady: "No man has ever seen me sitting with my legs crossed at my knee as women do nowadays. I was differently educated. My mother told me that a nice girl has both her feet on the ground."

61. A strange conception of sexuality was voiced by a college girl whom an older friend had advised to consult me. The girl told me quite casually that she had been in-

discriminately promiscuous since her eighteenth year. After I had expressed my astonishment that a well-bred and carefully brought-up girl should be so indifferent about her sexual attitude, she said: "I have often thought about it and I can perhaps explain how it came about. When I was a little girl, I was sent to Italy from where my family came and I spent my teen-age in a nunnery. I often played with myself and the nuns, who were very severe, told me that it is a deadly sin to play with oneself, even to touch oneself, and I would land in hellfire if I continued doing that. Their threats made a tremendous impression on me. When I left the nunnery, I sometimes felt sexually aroused and let myself be picked up by boys. Going to bed with them appeared to be less sinful."

62. Young girl: "I tried to make him talk about the possibility of marrying me, but he said almost nothing. It was more difficult to bring him to talk about it than tooth-pulling."

63. Woman criticizing her psychoanalyst: "Even your spontaneity in the analytic sessions is artificial."

64. This view of another woman's behavior was expressed by her woman friend: "She is working on this man and has, I believe, planned certain tactics for various situations. I think she will carry out a sneak attack on him like the Japs did at Pearl Harbor. He does, of course, not know that she contemplates marrying him. While she still cultivates diplomacy, he will be taken by surprise and will find himself engaged."

65. Young girl: "If I were to be truthful with my family, I would have to leave home."

66. College girl, enthusiastic about her teacher, to her girl friend: "You know, he speaks so well and it is as if he spoke to me all the time. I love him so and I could imagine that I let him . . . you know what."

67. Young widow: "I know, I have one smile for women and another for men."

68. Promiscuous woman, to her lover: "No one treats me with such lack of consideration as you and I do not know why I enjoy it so much from you and not from others."

69. College girl to another: "You know I am still a virgin and I am twenty-one. Sometimes it appears to me as if I had a physical handicap."

70. College girl to her boy friend: "I can go a long time without sex, but not without love."

71. Girl whose divorced mother has remarried: "Mother visited me yesterday and I asked her whether she loved my stepfather. You know what she answered? 'How can I love him? He is such a *nebbish*, a weakling.'"

"Mother neglects herself terribly. She had runs in her stockings, her blouse had some dirty spots, and she was not properly combed."

72. Girl: "All girls can occasionally be catty, but she is a wildcat."

73. Gossiping woman about another: "She is a real lady and only her enemies whisper that she is promiscuous. As a matter of fact, I know she is not—or rather within certain bounds. She was recently in Paris and on the French Riviera with her husband. When she returned, she told her women friends that she had arrived at an irrevocable decision. She said she would definitely limit the number of her lovers during her whole life to forty. Why just forty, you will ask? She had heard that this is the number of the members of the Academy of the Institute in France. She called them *les quarante immortels* and she said she wanted to make the men who slept with her feel immortal because of her lovemaking."

74. Girl who had an affair with a married man: "When I

thought of his wife, I felt ashamed of myself and guilty toward her. The part of being the 'other woman' I played then was loathsome to me. Besides that, I was almost sure that I was not alone the 'other woman,' but only one of the other women that man had. When I was not around, I had an understudy."

75. About another married woman: "Sure, she takes walks with her husband every evening after dinner. But it is as if she would walk a dog whose leash she does not loosen."

76. An observation on the variations of the sexes: "I sometimes catch myself on the street looking at the shoes, the stockings, and the skirts of a woman walking before me. Men always look at the legs of women, but I am interested in what kind of shoes they wear and in the cut of their skirts."

77. About her trip to Europe: "I was at Salzburg at the festival there. I think someone should now write a play called *Everywoman*. Women also have their typical experiences: first love, marriage, childbirth and before all, all husbands get fed up with them and tired of them and have affairs with other women."

"After I discovered that my husband had had quite a few affairs, I flirted with the fantasy of taking a lover. And why not? 'What's sauce for the gander is sauce for the goose.' But I am really a goose—I mean as stupid as a goose. I could not have an extramarital affair."

78. "Women always know what the score is with a man, but they often do not know how they know it and why."

79. Older, experienced woman: "The imprint of the first man left in a woman's sexual life is indelible, whoever he was. It is as if a traveler sets his foot on an unknown island that no one has trod before."

"When a young man and a young woman have frequent

dates, usually only one of them foresees whether they will marry—namely the young woman."

80. At the end of this part, dealing with the attitude of women to other women, I am, by way of exception, quoting a saying not of a patient but of Mrs. Freud. I once accompanied the old lady on a walk on the Semmering, a summer resort near Vienna. Sigmund Freud's wife was an excellent wife and mother and a kind person, but occasionally she could drop a malicious remark. She spoke of her family and said: "I get along famously with my two daughters-in-law. I never see them."

III Women about men

1. Immanuel Kant stated two hundred fifty years ago that woman does not reveal her secret. She does not even give it away easily in psychoanalytic sessions—except when she is not aware of self-revelation, which is, fortunately, often enough.

In the following pages you will find many such self-revelations—especially about the sexual life of women, so different from that of men—and many of these sayings give insights more penetrating than the Kinsey reports. The sexual aspect is, however, only one of the sides here considered; there is also the romantic and dependent attitude toward men, and even the maternal one. The critical side is, of course, not omitted.

Perhaps it would be appropriate to preface the following portion of this book by the remarks of a professor of psychology, made during training psychoanalysis. These remarks are perhaps not typical, but they show in quick succession the usual male conceit with regard to the understanding of women and the resignation that inevitably follows.

The man said: "I saw yesterday a new book entitled *When Women Look at Men* in the window. I suppose it is an anthology of the views of female writers on men. It is

obvious that women think much more about men than
men about women. But do women really think about men?
I mean, *think* in the full meaning of the word. I believe
they feel more, have rather an intuitive understanding of
men than a rational, clear, psychological comprehension."
He paused, then continued: "Yet sometimes one is inclined to believe that their intuitive understanding can be
more valuable than our trying to understand women in
terms of psychology. I have read some erudite books on
the emotional life of women and these books, written by
eminent psychologists, say a lot of nonsense. We really
don't understand what makes women tick. They remain
strange creatures, really strangers even when you have
lived with them many years in close intimacy."

Women perhaps sometimes wonder about men, but they
almost never consider them hopelessly inscrutable and
mysterious beings.

2. Here are a few instances of women's astonishment
about men's behavior in sexual situations: "My husband
quoted a Latin proverb to me yesterday. I cannot repeat
it, but it says that every man—or is it animal?—is sad
after sexual intercourse. But my husband is not sad after
it, only irritable and impatient with me."

3. "He never speaks to me before it, also not after it. He
could just as well be mute. Last Saturday it occurred to
me in the middle of lovemaking how a woman would feel
having intercourse with a man whose language she does
not understand. It was funny, but I thought that the man
could at least make some wooing noises."

4. Another kind of astonishment can be recognized in
the report of a young woman: "I occasionally saw, of
course, in my teens male genitals when the boys in school
were naughty, but I first saw the erected penis on my

wedding night. I still remember that I thought: 'Oh boy, how shall I ever get such a big thing inside me?' "

"It always astonishes me that it is first so small and weak and when I touch it, it gets to be as big as Goliath."

5. Married woman about a man who is making a play for her: "My impression is that he tests me. He sometimes tells me very risqué stories when he is alone with me. It is as if he wanted to find out how far he can go with me or how far is too far."

6. Woman in her late forties about her husband: "What hurts my feelings more than anything is his hypocrisy. When we are alone together, he never says anything nice to me. He just makes sarcastic or nasty remarks. But in the moment people come in, he calls me 'Darling' or 'Honey' and he holds my hand or puts his arm around me when we sit together."

7. A woman about her husband: "When we are at parties, he makes suggestive remarks to other women and almost propositions them in my presence. I wish he would sleep with one of them. I would prefer that to his public behavior. He seems not to feel how he humiliates me and hurts my feelings by his demonstrativeness to other women. . . ." Ten minutes later: "He behaved the same way yesterday at the party. When we came home late, I knew, of course, that he wanted me to come into his bed, but I have my pride too. If he wants something, he should come to me."

8. A married woman who is having an affair: "I came home late and after dinner my husband stroked my hair and kissed me. It happens very rarely. It is as if someone gives you a gift you don't like. You hate it because you feel that he expects you to be grateful to him and you cannot be."

9. Rather naïve young girl who has fallen in love: "I am so silly. I am often trying out how his name and mine sound together. And I imagine other things, together, of course. Is that what they call trial marriage?"

10. Forty-year-old woman about a man with whom she is having an affair: "I wonder about him. In sex he is like instant coffee. Immediately ready to use."

"His hands went astray, but they arrived at the place where he wanted them to go."

11. Man in his early fifties: "After dinner yesterday my wife and I had a serious conversation about our sexual life together. It gets worse and worse. Whenever I somehow express the desire to have a sexual party and when she does not have one of her headaches or is not too tired, she goes to the bathroom to put her diaphragm in. She stays in there a long time. . . . Yesterday when she came out from there and lay down, she casually remarked that it would help her if I could read poetry to her before it— she meant before lovemaking. Did you ever hear anything like that? Imagine: first going to the bathroom and me waiting for her and then I should read poetry to her! I ask you 'What man can wait so long?' "

The psychoanalyst agreed with the patient about the difficulty of sustaining an erection for such a long time, but tried to find an explanation for the behavior of his wife. Perhaps he did not have enough affectionate prelude before sexual intercourse with her, I said. Most women need to be wooed in the same manner; they want to be admired and want to be told that you love them and wish to hear sweet words from the man. Reading poetry to her, I declared, was perhaps for her a poor substitute for wooing her. If he would be more affectionate with her before the sexual act the reading would be superfluous, I added. "What do you mean," the patient indignantly said. "I am perhaps not demonstrative enough: Yesterday when my wife passed by me in the kitchen, I gave her a pat on her behind."

12. A woman about her husband: "He came to me with great passion. But then suddenly 'London Bridge was falling down.'" At another session: "My husband has developed such a passion for riding and horses that I thought he would be happier if he could live in a stable like Gulliver when he returned from his voyage to the Houyhnhnms." The same woman: "I know that there are men who have three or four sexual affairs at the same time. I do not understand how they go about it. Perhaps they need only a certain skill, like coachmen who drive a vehicle with four or five horses."

13. Young woman married for two months, about her husband: "He is so passionate and he wants to make love every night. I am afraid that his sexual desire will be suddenly deflated like a balloon."

14. "My husband always complains about the time I need for dressing and makeup and I tell him 'If you want that done quickly, you should have married a man, not a woman.'"

15. Woman about men in sexual situations: "The main thing is that a man should not give a woman time to think when he makes love to her. When a man hesitates, stops kissing me or touching me, I want to shout 'Don't stop! Please, don't stop.' I want him to continue, no interruptions, no pauses. It is ridiculous, for instance, to ask me questions at this point."

16. Middle-aged woman about a married couple: "The husband knows, of course, that his wife has a lover, but this seems not to bother him. She is a very good cook. Of the community of table and bed he obviously prefers the first part."

17. "It is difficult for a woman to ignore the glance of a man passing her on the street, but quite easy to pretend that she is not aware of it."

18. A college girl about herself: "I had sexual intercourse with one man and then with another man the next week. Sometimes I appear to myself like the whore of Babylon. Yet what I really want is to be a one-man woman." The same girl at another time: "A stupid woman understands more about the ways of men than wise men will ever know about the manners of women."

19. "Since I know about my husband's affair, I sometimes think of taking a lover. But I shudder at the thought that I would have to begin again to get accustomed to a kind of conjugal intimacy: dressing, undressing, and going to the bathroom before a man."

20. Woman in her early forties about her absent lover: "I have often wondered about him since he went to Argentina with this business contract. He will stay there for two months. I am convinced that he will sleep with another woman within a week. Why is that so with men? Have they no heart, no memory, no feelings that continue? A woman cannot do this; she cannot change her lover as she changes her dresses. Often I think of him while he is away. He is not only on my mind, but also in my body, in my blood."

21. Married woman about a sexual adventure: "He fell asleep afterwards. I got up from bed and went over to his jacket. I found a letter from California, from his wife. Now I know he is married." The same woman: "My husband is not very potent any longer. I help him as much as I can, of course, but . . . You know what people say, 'You can take a horse to the water, but you cannot make it drink.'"

22. Middle-aged woman: "Most men know as little about the sexuality of the women with whom they sleep as

the passengers of a railway compartment know about the engine that moves their train."

"You don't need to be a sorceress to change men into swine. All you need is sex appeal."

23. Another woman: "I believe my husband expects sexual intercourse as a reward after he has told me of a good business deal."

"He makes love as mechanically as if my body were a sex machine or a computer."

24. Romantic feelings are awakened in a young girl who says: "I have been in a serious depression since my boy friend and I talked about our not being able to get married. I must, of course, pretend that I am independent of him, which I don't really feel. I often catch myself being morbidly preoccupied with him in my thoughts and waiting for the telephone to ring."

25. Young girls sometimes find themselves in situations that embarrass them: "At the dance last evening was a nice young man whom I did not know but whom I liked. I looked at him and he looked at me and sometimes our glances met. I hoped that he would come over to me, speak to me, and ask me to dance with him. But he didn't. He seemed to be bashful. What could I do? I could not get a flag and wave it, could I?"

The same young girl on a later occasion: "I wished to call him and to ask him to meet me somewhere in mid-Manhattan. I wished he would take me to dinner or to a dance. I dialed his number and I heard his voice and then my courage failed me. I hung up. I just could not do it, but felt happy to hear his voice."

The same a few weeks later: "He kissed me and then I kissed him. In the middle of our petting I was worried whether my hem looked uneven."

"Before I went away to college, my mother repeatedly

told me 'The first duty of a nice girl in company of men is to keep her skirts down.'"

26. Mature woman: "When all is done in bed together, not all is said. You understand don't you?"

"I was married to him for one year. What was sex like with him, you ask? The less said about it, the better . . . and there was very little to say about it."

27. A woman speaking about a man who had been her lover: "When I think of him now, I don't feel the slightest excitement any longer. I don't even remember having been aroused with him then. The well has dried up."

28. Woman about her sex life: "No, I do not always experience an orgasm, but sometimes he brings me that far, and then I give of my substance as a bee gives honey."

29. Woman speaking of her wedding: "When we came home after the wedding I threw my arms around him and he recoiled. I have now been married more than twenty years and I have never done this again. I am, of course, frigid; I mean I am frigid with him, not with other men."

"My husband sometimes wanted to have sex with me and it happened that it was when I had just returned from the apartment of my lover. I had, of course, to yield to my husband, but I couldn't care less."

"A man is the only animal that likes to be chased."

"All men are the same. They all want to go to bed with a woman as soon as possible."

30. Middle-aged woman, refugee from Nazi Germany: "I catch myself sometimes humming a little tune my mother often sang. It's from an old Berlin operetta:

'*Die Männer sind alle Verbrecher*
Aber lieb, aber lieb sind sie doch.'

[Men are criminals altogether,
But they are darlings, such darlings.]

31. Patient speaking of the appointment she had had with a physician the day before: "I told the doctor my whole story. My mouth felt so dry that I asked whether I could get a glass of water. I expected, of course, that he would bring it to me like a gentleman. But he only pointed to the faucet and to the glasses. When I went over there, I had the distinct feelings that he looked at my legs."

32. Married woman describes the visit she had paid to a bachelor: "I was in his apartment more than two hours. He gave me some wine and we talked about many things —about ourselves too. I told him that I am not happy in my marriage. He said that he loved me. We then petted and kissed a long time. When I looked at the clock, I saw to my terror that it was high time to return home. I wanted to be there when my husband came from his office. I had to put my make-up on in a hurry. . . . Later on, at home, I remembered our long petting party and I regretted that there had not been time to get better acquainted."

The same woman speaks of two kinds of man she had met lately. About one she says: "He is fifty years old, but in approaching women he is as bashful as a high school boy." About the other: "He has no friends, but he runs after all girls. He is what they call a lone wolf. In any event, he is a wolf."

About her marriage: "Our wedding night was the anticlimax to our engagement and love story."

Speaking of parties: "Men are funny. When you flirt with them in all innocence, just for the sake of flirting, they consider that the promise of an affair."

Several months later: "I was fed up with my husband

and I wanted a casual affair with that musician. But after we had made love a few times, I really fell in love with him. It is not easy for a woman to have a casual affair. Men have it much better in this direction."

"Women sometimes express feelings they don't experience at all persuasively and they carefully hide other feelings they really feel. . . . Men are so gullible. Their simple-mindedness astonishes me again and again. . . . It is much more difficult for a woman than for a man to be honest."

33. The following paragraphs—written, as were all the other notes, after psychoanalytic sessions, often in the pauses between them—follow the development of the love affair of a college girl. The notes cover, of course, several months. At the same time her sayings furnish us rare insights into her emotional life:

"As every girl in her twenties is, I was sometimes frightened by the ghost of spinsterhood. The threat of becoming an old, bitter virgin hung over my head like a sword of Damocles. . . . I was sometimes offended and ashamed of the thoughts I read in the eyes of men looking at me on the streets. Yet when they did not pay any attention to me, I was even more offended.

"When I talked with John, I was often quite touched by his puerility. He was such a boy! He took everything I said very seriously—you know all those silly things a girl sometimes says. He was also very upset when I changed my mind. He looked at me then as if he could not understand me at all.

"After we were sexually together, I always think of him. My girl friend tells me I should behave more aloofly when I am with him and that's no good. But I cannot help it and he knows.

"Speaking of first sexual intercourse with that young man: I took off my dress and my bra and stretched myself out on his bed and waited for him and for an instant I thought of myself as of the animal sacrifice on the altar.

"He got up after it was over and looked at me as I was lying there nude and I got very embarrassed because I did not know what kind of impression I made lying naked in bed and I covered myself with the sheets. He laughed.

"In the pauses between our lovemaking he sometimes behaved as if he had forgotten my presence and I once asked him 'Where are you in your thoughts?' but he did not answer me.

"I sometimes provoked a quarrel with him because I looked forward to a reconciliation which I brought about. He was then sometimes affectionate with me.

"He became worried because I had not had my period for six weeks. He asked me again about it and I said: 'It's later than you think.'

"He said we must be reasonable. My girl friend tells me that men always say 'Let's be reasonable' when they want to make an end.

"He could find pretext and shifts and he could lie almost as casually and ingeniously as a woman.

"When he left me on our last date, he kissed me on the cheek as if I were a child. I was tempted to ask whether he should not also give me a pat on the head.

"I often think of him now. No man can love a girl the same way a girl loves a man.

"Sexual intercourse lasts only a short time. Then the man leaves you and you're again alone as before.

"A few months later a nice young man wooed me with great eagerness. It gave me pleasure to torture him. I took revenge on him for the grief John caused me when he did not love me any longer and turned to that other woman. At the same time I knew I was cruel toward the new man and felt guilty for it."

34. Married woman: "The best thing a wife can do for her husband, when they are in company, is to put him into the limelight."

35. An actress, about an emotional change in herself: "I was in Hollywood two years and became quite masculine in some directions. It did, of course, not go so far that I unlearned some feminine ways such as gossiping, shopping, flirting."

36. A career girl: "I sometimes visit the girls with whom I had been in college. Most of them are now married and some have a child or even two. I envy them, of course. But the other day I saw Anne's husband looking at her with a kind of condescending smile when she bent down to pick up her baby and I thought 'This will not happen to me.' Of course, I want to have a baby too, but then I want to go back as soon as possible to my career. My husband should never look at me that way, without respect for me."

37. Married woman in her early forties: "You don't know how often women who are well provided for think of widowhood. I mean how often they enjoy the promise of future widowhood—even when they are quite fond of their husbands. They then anticipate a future of all kinds of potentialities. They daydream about it as a young single girl looks forward to married life. The other day I had a tiff with my husband and felt depressed. And then I caught myself at the fantasy of being a 'merry widow.'"

The same woman, about an emotional difference of the sexes: "Jealousy makes a man blind and dumb. He wants to find the truth as a bull wants to find and to attack the red cloth that offends him or fills him with rage. A woman who is jealous is first of all not as sincere about it as a man. She conceals it and she is clever and often discovers the truth in an indirect and ingenious manner, sometimes by discreet questions. In my eyes Othello is a fool. If Desdemona had been jealous, she would have become a genius in fact-finding."

38. The mother of two children: "I really don't know what happened then, only that this man—my lover—gave me my first orgasm—after I had been married to Ben for almost ten years. All this time I had been frigid. I knew, of course, that the other man was inferior to Ben in every direction. And I loved my husband. Yet I saw in the lover a kind of magician who could perform a miracle when he gave me those deeply satisfying orgasms. That occurred every time I was with him. He was a kind of redeemer in my eyes then. I was ready to leave Ben and even my children and to go with him wherever he wanted me to go."

39. Woman telling the story of her marriage: "In the first week of our honeymoon he often made love to me, as he called it in an overstatement. I woke up in the morning, thinking of what had occurred in the night, and saying to myself 'There must be more to life than this.' . . . After sexual intercourse he gets up immediately and goes to the bathroom to wash himself. Does he think that I am dirty or make him dirty? I then feel deeply hurt. The thought of what follows our so called 'lovemaking' was often there before it and I was not lubricated. I was as dry as that wood of your desk. . . . When I became pregnant and it had become visible, my husband did not want to go out with me to a concert or even a restaurant. It was as if he was ashamed of my being so big."

40. Married woman who had entered an extramarital affair: "He took me to a cheap hotel and when I looked at

the walls, the furniture, and the bed after we had sexual intercourse, I felt cheap myself and I felt guiltier toward my husband because of those shabby surroundings. But it did not bother my lover at all. It was as if he were entirely unaware of the surroundings and saw only me. . . . When I came home, my husband asked me where I had been and why I was so late. I told him that I was with a woman friend and had not noticed how late it was as we had chatted. . . . I remember a time when I still knew that I was lying to him. Now I sometimes don't realize any longer whether I lie or tell the truth. He does not lie to me and if he once in a while tries to, poor fellow, I see through it immediately."

41. College girl: "When I came to the party, quite a few young fellows were introduced to me and I looked them over. I suddenly thought of a cafeteria not far from Columbia University where I had dinner several times when it became too late to cook at home. In the cafeteria you go from one window to the next and choose the dish you like. I looked in the same manner at the fellows at the party and I asked myself: 'Which one should I choose —cafeteriawise you know.' " On another occasion: "Before going out, I looked at myself and at my dress and observed how it hung smoothly down to the hem. I sometimes wonder whether men also look down at their pants this way."

The same girl, about a recent experience: "We took a walk together in the evening in the park. It had already begun to get dark. He suddenly embraced me and kissed me. I was frightened for a moment and pushed him back. He told me later on that I had said then 'Jesus, Maria, and Joseph!' I did not remember that I had cried that, only that I was taken by surprise as if by a sudden attack. He said too that he had concluded from my outcry that I was

Catholic. He is Jewish, you know, but my being Catholic did not disturb him in the least. . . . We walked and talked and I knew that he would kiss me again, but now, I was, of course, prepared for it and wished he would do it. More than this, while we talked, I began to count, one, two, three because I was curious when he would kiss me. . . . He later on called me a sweet girl. I did not say anything—what could one say?—but I knew that I was not a sweet girl at all and that he sees me as someone I am not."

42. Girl who is secretary in a law firm: "I asked Nelson to wait until the evening, but he said, 'What's wrong with a matinée and an evening performance too?' I had to yield and we went to bed in the afternoon. In the evening, he said he felt tired. There was, of course, no evening performance. When I got up in the morning, I saw to my dismay that I had a long run in my stockings. He said 'That's no calamity,' but I could not possibly appear in the office like this. It was already late because I had overslept and I had to run. My only hope was that I would find a hosiery store open so early where I could buy some seamless nylons. Fortunately I saw one. The salesgirl opened it just when I passed there and she allowed me to put on the stockings in the store."

43. Mature woman about a bachelor: "He was hitching his wagon to a star—I mean a movie star, of course."

44. A young woman about another: "She sometimes has delusions of not being persecuted by men any more. At those times of her nonpersecution mania she is very depressed."

45. "Don't fool yourself, a woman in a restaurant or on the street has seen you long before you have seen her and she has prepared herself in her attitude or posture for the moment you will see her."

46. There is something typically feminine in this woman's attitude: "I was gently stroking my body the way James did and I became aroused vicariously remembering him. I don't understand people who write novels about love and sex. I experience them in my imagination. Is this not enough? Why do they need to write them down?

"Since James left me, I like to hear my women friends talk about their lovers. Listening to them, I get the impression I am hearing an echo of my own experiences."

47. Patient speaking to her psychoanalyst: "When you listen to me a long time without saying anything, I often have the impression that what I say is silly woman's stuff and without value. It is as if you do not consider it worth your while to speak to me."

The same girl after having been in psychoanalytic treatment several months: "Yesterday I had a dream and I could interpret it myself in the morning when I woke up. It was Sunday, so I did not have to get up early and all kinds of thoughts occurred to me. I had dreamed that I was going uptown to the laundry. When I arrived there, I unpacked my linen and underwear and was astonished how much dirty stuff I had. It was much more than I had thought and there were even a few pieces I did not immediately recognize as my own. Now, my laundry is not uptown, but in my street—but your office is uptown. When I was lying in bed, I thought that I'll come to my psychoanalytic session on Monday. I am washing my dirty things in this office. It is true that I often am astonished how many unclean thoughts I have and that I sometimes hesitate to recognize some thoughts as my own."

"When I was twenty-one, I got into an affair with the druggist on the corner of Ninth Street. He was married and had two children and he ran after women. I then some-

times imagined what my girl friends would say about me
—'the company she keeps!' "

48. Woman in her forties: "Compliments from men?
One likes to hear them, but one does, of course, not believe
them. Yet I sometimes go to the mirror to find out whether
a compliment paid to me is true."

49. Married woman: "I deny it to myself that I am
sometimes sexually aroused by thinking of a certain man.
Can men do that too?"

"My husband and I had a violent quarrel that evening.
In the night he came over to me. He wanted to become
reconciled with me, but I could not lubricate and I did not
give a damn whether he came or not. When I love him I
want to feel his wetness, but not this time."

"I asked several people whether men also sometimes cry
themselves to sleep. I don't believe it."

50. Girl in her late twenties, still a virgin: "I listened to
the record of *My Fair Lady* yesterday evening. Then I
went to bed, but I could not fall asleep. That waltz tune
'I Could Have Danced All Night' haunted me. I could not
get rid of that melody. It suddenly occurred to me that the
word *danced* is perhaps a substitute for another word. I'll
not tell you the vulgar expression I thought of. Then the
tune did not pursue me any longer and I fell asleep."

51. Girl about her boy friend, who is in another city:
"You know, he wrote me that I am the only oasis in the
desert of his life up there."

The same girl, about another college boy: "He reads only
escape literature, novels and such stuff. I think he wants
to escape from himself."

The same girl two years later, about her boy friend: "I
often thought how I could force him to marry me. For instance I thought I could make a tiny hole in his rubbers

with a fine needle. I would perhaps become pregnant then. But that was more than a year ago. Now he bores me to tears."

52. Young girl: "While I gave some clever answer to his questions and sweetly smiled at his compliments, I looked at his hands and imagined how it would feel to be touched by him."

53. Returning from a voyage to Europe, a college girl reports: "When we came to the French border the customs man wanted me to open one of my bags. I was so embarrassed because all my underwear was in it. And he being French. . . ."

The same girl, speaking about earlier years: "My mother bought me my first bra and I remember how proud I was of it and of my little breasts. They were not so little either. Some boys in school made remarks about them."

54. Older, experienced woman advising young woman: "Play-acting becomes a necessity for women in certain situations with men, nearly to the extent that she does not know which is her first nature. . . . Every woman must be at least a little of a bitch. . . ."

55. Woman recounting the story of her unhappy marriage: "He was a typical New Englander and expressed highly idealistic views about love. I was, of course, frigid with him because I was ashamed before him and would not let myself go. I was always troubled by the idea 'What would he think of me?' I then had several affairs in which I was not frigid at all."

56. Wife to her husband: "You have a marked talent for always saying the wrong thing to me or saying things at the wrong time."

57. Young woman confiding to a friend: "I heard he had said about me 'She has the mind of a child.' Now I ask you, should I consider this a compliment or an insult?"

58. Woman about a man she had met: "Everybody knows that he is attracted by forbidden fruits. He had plenty of affairs with married women. Someone said of him the other day that he just likes the apples in another man's garden."

59. There is a core of truth in the complaint made by a middle-aged woman during a psychoanalytic session: "Men are odd. They do not permit us to be only women; I mean women with all their moods and weaknesses; but they do not let us for a moment forget that we are only women."

60. Girl who studies German language and literature at college: "I tried to translate Schiller's *Das Lied von der Glocke* yesterday. Anne who comes from Germany helped me. I arrived at the line

> '*Mit dem Gürtel, mit dem Schleier*
> *Reisst der schöne Wahn entzwei.*'

Do you speak German? Let me translate it for you:

> 'With the girdle, with the veil
> The beautiful illusion is torn to pieces.'

"I thought at first it meant that love ends for the man when he has deflowered the girl. But Anne told me that it meant that the illusion of love is destroyed in the wedding night. If it would only last so long! I know some girls who yielded to the man and he deserted them then without marrying them. If he stays with you and loves you so long and he leaves you then, you are at least a married woman."

61. Young woman: "I read a marriage manual the other day. Those manuals were mostly written by men and I was astonished what great part the authors attribute to the sexual adjustment of the woman. They don't say that a

man must adjust sexually to the woman too. While I was reading that marriage manual a funny comparison occurred to me. I also know how it came to mind. My husband and I were at a symphony concert the evening before. I looked then at the concertmaster of the Philharmonic. He looked tired and I thought: 'What happens to him when he gets old or cannot play the fiddle so well? He will, of course, be put into the group of the second violins and another man will take his place.' Don't you think that husbands also should be replaced by younger men and put into the group of second violins?"

62. Woman in her forties: "You know I studied psychology and I almost made my M.A., but then I met my husband and we got married. It's not even funny any more, but I have observed again and again that a woman loses her ambition as soon as she marries."

63. An example of the sensitiveness of women. A young woman coming for a consultation was hesitant to speak. I asked her why she was unwilling to confide in me. She said: "When you opened the door to the waiting room and told me to come in, you did not smile at me."

64. College girl, discussing a student: "I thought of this boy when I read a newspaper article about Congress. The commentator said that Congress this year talks a lot but does little. You know, that boy who has been taking me out all these weeks and talks all the time about sex, he just kissed me a few times and once timidly touched my breasts."

65. Women in general do not swear or use four-letter words in psychoanalytic sessions. Here is an exception. The patient had been silent for a longer time than usual and then said in a quiet manner: "Goddam, I don't know why I am here. Fuck yourself!"

Another exception. A young girl angrily says: "Oh balls, as my brother forbade me to say."

66. Married woman: "After Henry left for his office this morning, I thought what I should give him for dinner tonight. I thought: pea soup, breaded veal with spinach and salad, and then sex. I assure you, I thought of it as if it were a dessert such as a cake or a fruit cup. I imagine it was as if I were a mother preparing some dish a little boy likes especially."

The same woman on another occasion: "Men take sex too seriously—and sometimes not seriously enough."

67. Mature woman telling about her first love in high school: "The next time I ran into him, I was in dungarees and looked away. I hoped that he would not see me. If I had at least had my date dress on. . . . Then we had our first date. I was so eager that I came too early to the place and I was afraid of what he would think of that. I went into a bookstore nearby and looked at the new paperbounds, always glancing at the street. He came soon. After I had let him wait a few minutes, I came out from the store.

"I then took out my compact and while I powdered myself, watched him."

68. College girl: "I tried my best to make him fall in love with me and I made so desperate an effort that I fell in love with him myself."

"A girl who says to a man 'I look a mess' wants him to tell her that she looks very pretty."

69. Woman about her married life: "I did my best to make our marriage go, but with every move we were stuck in hopeless mud."

70. A married woman suspicious that her husband is unfaithful to her: "No woman in America knows what a

man does with all his time—even when he declares he has
no minute free."

71. A widow: "It is terribly cold in my apartment in
spite of the heating. The only place in which I feel warm
is the bed—and even there it is cool when I am alone in
it."

"A friend gave me the address of an excellent coiffeur.
I went there and when I looked at myself afterwards, I
asked myself 'Will he marry me when I have this new
hairdo?'"

"To be in love can be a full-time job for a woman, like
that of a profession for a man."

"You know that the first glance a woman casts at another one is to find out whether the other has a wedding
ring on. No use to look at a man's finger for that. Either he
is married and does not wear a wedding ring or, if he does,
his wife is with him and you need not look."

72. Single woman: "Any eligible bachelor who does not
want to be married awakens in me the hunting instinct—
sometimes only for a moment. . . . The male is the only
animal that likes to be chased. . . ."

The same woman about a certain young man: "He did
not talk of loving me or even feeling attracted to me, but
he took me out very frequently. I waited and waited in
vain. It is very exhausting for a girl to be so patient.

"I cannot get him to bed. I know that is a strange
complaint for a girl. Very few women could complain
about that; when they set their minds on this, they always
succeed. I asked myself 'Why do I fail?' He is not
a eunuch. He is not married. It seems he has no mistress.
What does he do with his sexuality? It's too awful to think
that he could be homosexual or find satisfaction with himself."

73. Mature woman: "Men often don't notice the sur-

roundings when they first enter an apartment; women always do."

"Women of the same age group are always competitive. They look at each other with envy or contempt and sometimes with a mixture of both. And they know it too. All those sweet words like 'Darling' and 'Dear' and 'Honey' cannot deceive us about our basic hostility toward one another."

"When you listen intelligently to a man talking of his own interests and sometimes pose an appropriate question, his temptation to show off to you becomes very strong."

74. Married woman who is having an extramarital affair says of her husband: "I sometimes feel guilty toward him and I resent this feeling he awakens in me. I then get in a bad mood and begin to nag him."

75. Married woman about her lover: "At that party I said something that was destined only for him, but I said it before all the people there and I enjoyed the fact that none of them had the slightest notion what it meant to us two."

"I looked at him and said: 'Where are you in your thoughts?' and I suspected that he thought of his wife. Then I decided I would not sleep with him that day."

76. Young woman: "I know, when I feel awful I look awful to my husband and then I cannot stand it when he kisses me. It is as if he does not love me, but feels sorry for me."

77. About her eighteen-year-old niece: "You know what she said last week? 'All men are selfish, inconsiderate, and brutal and I wish I would find one.'"

78. Woman coming late to the psychoanalytic session, breathlessly telling the reason for her lateness: "What happened? I closed the door of my apartment and did not

know that I left the key to it and my money inside. I had to borrow two dollars from the elevator man to pay for the taxi to come over here. . . . Maybe I did not want to come today."

79. Young woman: "I don't understand the feelings of men. My husband has me. Why does he need other women? What do they have that I haven't got?"

80. Advice given by an older woman to a girl: "So long as you are engaged, you must always listen to what the man says. Once you're married, it is enough that you pretend to listen to him."

81. College girl: "I sometimes think that all men are sex-crazy or sex-starved. All they think about when they are with a young girl is going to bed with her."

82. Women about a man who took her out several times: "At first he bored me, but later he became quite interesting and some things he said were just fascinating. After I left him the last time, it occurred to me that it is quite similar to my response to certain musical pieces when I was a little girl. When I heard Bach for the first time, I thought his music bored me, but I heard the same piece later on on a record and I felt it beautiful. Certain things you acknowledge only at the second or third hearing."

83. Middle-aged woman about her husband: "He has no friends and he kills any offering of human kindness; he makes outlandish remarks and mows people down. I know, of course, that he is deeply insecure and needs a lot of reassurance. . . . The need to be loved is perhaps felt more deeply by those who pretend that they don't give a damn about other people."

84. Woman about her husband: "I know, he is a poor thing, but my own."

About another man: "I rang up and they sent me someone to help me furnish the new apartment. He was, of course, an interior decorator and I never thought of him as of a man."

85. "When I meet that type of strong, silent man, I have the impulse to soften him and to see him reduced to the point that I feel he is very attracted to me."

86. About a couple: "They have nothing in common any longer but sex."

87. Refugee from Austria: "There was a lady in Vienna whose bons mots circulated in the city. She once said about a certain man 'Sleeping with him, yes—but no intimacies.'"

"You would think that the intentions of a woman who makes advances to a man are obvious. But it is not so. Sometimes she is only teasing him and sometimes only testing her power over him. Yes, sometimes she even wants to frustrate him at the critical moment. Sexual intercourse can be a hostile act of the woman."

"We sometimes lie because we are embarrassed and lie not to embarrass others. There are lies to conceal something and lies to find something out about others."

88. A woman to her friend: "He asked me with whom I had slept while he was on that business trip and I said: 'Look who is asking!'—Do you know that he is violently jealous? He does not want me to go out with any man or even with a girl friend."

89. Complaint of a young woman: "I sometimes ask myself: Have I nothing to offer a man other than this body? I can take care of him in all directions, as a cook and as a secretary, as housekeeper and financial adviser, as stimulating partner in conversation and as friend, as lady of the house as well as a maid. Yes, I can take care of him in all these regards, not only of his sexual needs."

90. I should like to conclude this part as I did the preceding one, with a memory of Mrs. Freud. I remember

that Freud and I were going down the stairs from his office in the Berggasse when it suddenly started to rain heavily. Mrs. Freud ran after her husband, crying "Your rubbers!"

IV Men

1 Men about women

1. All the conventions of Western civilization prevent men from speaking freely about their wives and mistresses. Only under the influence of many drinks do men sometimes confide in the bartender. There remains only one place where a man speaks his mind freely and uninhibitedly about that subject: the psychoanalyst's office. The analyst who listens to men and women for many hours observes several differentiating features in the content and the expression of their speech. Men do not mince words and frequently use four-letter expressions. The reader of the following pages will sometimes be subjected to the violent shock of words. Except when they are young, men speak less of love than women do, but much more about sex. Married life, which is for the average woman the harbor she enters as place of shelter, has for most men a different significance. Their relations with women are in the majority of cases governed by the fluctuations of male sexuality. Sexual intercourse has therefore a place in their life different from that women reserve for it. This is valid from the late teens, when sexual intercourse on the back seat of a car belongs to the initiation rites of manhood, until old age, in which physical desire becomes rare and cannot reach the stage of performance.

It would be most appropriate to begin this chapter by

quoting the words of various men concerning marriage and wife-troubles, but before we enter that area, I would like to insert here a few verses given me by their writer. The reader can enter the world of the male through this portal.

There is no rule without an exception. The rule adhered to in this volume is the anonymity of those quoted. The following doggerel, chosen from a rich collection, are the exception. Alan Abrons explicitly authorized me to name him as their writer. The first two pieces are attacks, the others reflect various moods of the author.

If a man's born deaf and dumb
Then a psychiatrist he should become
And he can sit and look profound
And never utter a single sound.

The pay is good, the girls are cute
And to be so mute seems quite astute
And nobody will ever find
That he has neither voice nor mind.

Penis envy is woman's lot
    While men are afraid to lose what they've got.
This is something it's hard to avoid
    At least according to Sigmund Freud.

For me it's hard to believe that Venus
    Was sorely vexed 'cause she lacked a penis.
Centuries of constant admiration
    Ought to make up for her deprivation.

Nor do I think men live in fear
    That their genitals will disappear.
I believe that men suppose
    That their penis will last as long as their nose.

Liquor and cigarettes are a curse
  When I indulge I couldn't feel worse;
Sex is costly, food puts on weight
  I think I'll call and cancel my date.

LAMENT OF A MALE TEEN-AGER (IN HIS 30s)

Girls are fearsome, worrysome, wearysome
  And oftentimes very tearysome
Yet deliriously, delightfully we pursue
  We lust and love and hate and screw
  (Well, what else can a young man do?)

Girls can be pretty, girls can be fat
  They can be sweet, or mean as a rat;
They can be quiet, they can be loud
  Can plunge you in misery, or make you float on a cloud.

Girls can be chaste, or quite promiscuous
  They can withhold, or give a kiss to us;
Girls can make love, and what is more yet,
  They can do what we can't, they can beget.

So since nothing better can be found
  At least we know that girls are around
Whether in bliss, or whether in strife
  Whether as mistress, or whether as wife
  Without them it wouldn't be much of a life.

Also the relationship of man to man is different from that women have with men. The following statements will show that the criticisms evoked are expressed directly and do not contain the sweet slow-working poison that is injected into remarks of women about other women. Also the verbal attacks of male patients against their psychoanalysts are in this characteristic manner open and direct.

2. Middle-aged man: "It's not true that women are not interested in ideas. They are not interested in abstract ideas, but they often personalize them or connect them with certain men in their minds."

3. Young man to his girl friend: "Thus we meet at eight-ten before the theatre. Maybe you will succeed in coming not later than is necessary for a woman who must dress and make up."

4. Young patient: "I had a strange experience on the bus on which I came over here yesterday. A woman wanted to step down after we had passed the bus stop. The driver looked at her when she complained that he did not stop, and said: 'Readiness is all, lady!' "

"Today I sat and looked, as usual, at the legs of women sitting across from me. There was a woman whose legs were so fat they reminded one of an elephant, and at the next station an older woman came in and sat down. Her legs were as thin as a lath. How much difference a few pounds more or less make in the impression a woman makes on a man."

5. Young man: "Love is social by nature, but sex is impersonal. This means there is no such thing as a social sex act. What we accomplish in sex is a fusion for some minutes, and after this is reached each person is again isolated. I don't deny that sexual intercourse tries to make two people one, but the result is simply the failure of a mission."

6. Man in his thirties: "In sexual intercourse I am always premature, I have a too-early emission which leaves me as well as her dissatisfied. I am, so to speak, 'trigger-unhappy!' "

The same man, speaking of his teens: "I was then very shy with girls. I considered them as something made from sugar and spice. Only later did I understand that also girls are beings of flesh and blood. About blood I found out because I saw the napkins of my older sister."

7. Patient: "I just rode on a bus that passed the apartment I lived in five years ago. I remembered the wonderful time I had there when Jane came up twice a week or as often as she could get away from her husband and child. We sometimes did not leave the bed the whole afternoon. Yet if I should meet her again, it would not be the same. I have changed and I am sure she has. Who knows how many lovers she has had in the meantime? No, it would not be the same any more. The memories I have kept are certainly more beautiful than the reality was."

8. Married man telling of a friend's visit the preceding evening: "When we were alone, Ben suggested that we should go to a brothel together later. He told me that he knew of a few beautiful girls there. My wife came in then and, when she saw me take my overcoat, asked me where I was going. I told her that Ben and I had to go to a business meeting and she asked whether she could come along. Did you ever hear such a thing? To take your wife to a brothel? It would be like carrying bad oil to Texas."

9. Young man: "I was sent to a lady psychoanalyst at first and had an interview with her. She was quite pretty and seemed nice. I told myself: 'To go to bed with her, yes, but to the couch, no.'"

"During the summer there was quite an exchange of husbands and wives among the young couples in that summer resort. I believe such exchanges are rarely successful. How do the French say? *Plus que ça change, plus c'est la même chose.*"

10. Young man about a girl: "We went to bed. I was astonished how experienced that girl was. First finger exercises before she began real work."

11. Old man in consultation: "As far as feeling sexual

desire at all, we old men prefer the women to be sexually active and take the initiative. But we still remember that we were once young and would prefer to have the attitude of young men."

"It is a world of relativity also with regard to the importance different people attach to various problems. The other day I listened to the conversation some women were having about a party to which they were invited and—you know—for a moment I had the impression that there is a female counterpart to the many political and sociological problems that vex the world, namely the question 'What should I wear?' "

"She sat down across from me in such a way that a considerable part of her underwear became visible. I didn't know whether she was careless or flirtatious."

12. Man about an actress: "She was, I think, over forty and she told me that no man had touched her before she was twenty-one years old. I bet she could become a virgin again at the drop of her hat."

13. "We went to her apartment and she said: 'Don't let's wait for the elevator. It's only three floors.' She went up the stairs very slowly before me. She is, of course, very proud of her legs."

About a girl unwilling to yield to him: "I did whatever I could to lay her, but in vain. Believe me, she is beautiful. My friend John tells me that I am always judging a book by its cover. Now, I ask you, by what else can you judge a book whose leaves you are not allowed to turn?"

14. Man: "You know, my wife gave me carte blanche sexually. I may go whenever and with whatever woman I want. What more can a philandering husband wish? It's strange; I want to return to the old situation, because I need that guiltiness, that particular furtiveness, that secrecy and the forbidden nature of sexual relations."

"I don't know why I opened *Hamlet* today. The prince accosts Ophelia with his question: 'Are you honest?' What a question to ask a girl! How should she know? No woman does."

"I just saw a young woman with a high hairdo à la Brigitte Bardot. The woman was rather petite and it looked ridiculous. Women are so silly that even dwarfs would follow that recent fashion of high hairdos."

15. Young man about a college girl who is studying psychology and who is especially interested in psychoanalysis: "Until recently our relations were quite good—touch wood. But she has already begun to analyze my unconscious motives and such things. I'm afraid a little more learning would be a dangerous thing."

The same man, about the same girl on a previous occasion: "You know what is the main precondition for lovemaking in her case? That the telephone should be off the hook, the light be turned off, the curtains carefully closed, and the door well bolted.

"She became pregnant. It was a chain accident. On that evening she came to me after she broke with her fiancé and after she had lost her job. She was especially passionate with me because she had had a quarrel with her parents the day before and she wanted to marry me as soon as possible.

"A few days later I took another girl to dinner and accompanied her home. I had known her for a few weeks and I kissed her in the dark hallway of her house and I pressed her body to me. She pushed me back and said 'I believe you want to rape me!' and I answered 'I confess it would be lovely.' "

16. Young man: "She came in, sat in a chair and pulled her skirt down. It was quite unnecessary since I did not feel attracted to her in the least."

"When she turned around, a little piece of her thighs became visible. She caught my glance and became as embarrassed as if I had surprised her in the act of stealing or picking her nose. . . ."

17. Old man: "When a young woman got up for me in the bus the first time and invited me to take her seat I was far from being grateful. I was on the contrary furious with her and felt like slapping her face. I guess I realized then finally that I was considered a really old man."

18. Young man: "After that girl had rejected me, I took a walk on Forty-Second Street. Very soon I did not think of her any longer, but I wanted to have a woman. Any woman, you understand."

19. Young man: "I remember having read somewhere the question: 'Is there such a being as a woman alone?' This makes sense to me because women always look at themselves with the eyes of another or many others. . . . A few months ago I had a strange image—I think you psychologists call these pictures hypnagogic because they emerge before falling asleep. Now in my studio there was a plastic terrestrial globe standing in the corner. In the twilight I saw that the globe had eyes and a mouth that was besmeared with lipstick. . . ."

The same man: "The art experts often speak of the beauty of movements. Only the other day I read an enthusiastic description of the antique statue of the Discobolus, that Greek youth throwing a discus. I don't see the beauty in it. You know what I consider the most beautiful movement in the world? When a woman is lying down and lifts her skirt for me—especially when she has nothing underneath."

"Sometimes I review my experiences with women before getting up in the morning. I see them then in images and I recognize that each woman has her peculiar traits in love-making. Each of them has, so to speak, her *spe-cialité de la maison.*"

"I stood just now before a dress shop and heard two women discuss a certain costume in the window. They spoke about the minutest details of it. I have never heard men speak of suits this way."

"Ernest considers the seduction of married women not only as pleasure, but almost his duty."

20. Bachelor: "I like the little noise when I snap a girdle."

"The girl has no pleasure in sexual intercourse. She only goes through the motions—and very few motions as they are."

About another girl: "During sex she is quite uninhibited, but she feels embarrassed afterwards when she dresses and asks me to wait in the other room."

"She reproached me and said that I make love as mechanically as if her body were a machine. She said she hated that. But later on she confessed that she—but only rarely—used me the same way."

About another woman: "She says she is a passionate legitimist and she does not want any affairs, but to be married."

21. Young man with potency disturbances: "I could not wait any longer in sexual intercourse and I let go. I had an emission. The bullet had left the gun and I did not know whether it was a hit or a miss."

22. Another patient: "I am restless and full of sexual desire. I wonder who will take care of me this evening, Jane or Anne."

"We made love without me feeling any love for her, of course. I just functioned sexually. It is perhaps necessary to fool the woman and to pretend that you love her, but why should I fool myself?"

23. Man, about a woman he saw at a party the day before: "Where other women have curves, she has forms that only a very modern architect could describe."

"She always says that she does not want to get 'physically involved.' Hell, what an expression!"

"She is very afraid of getting pregnant and insists that I withdraw before emission. This has gone on now for several weeks. I think this kind of intercourse is cruel and I call it woman's inhumanity to man. I begin to hate her."

"Roger is impotent not only with his wife—I would be too in his case—but also with other women."

24. Man in his late sixties: "When you get old, there remains only memories of sex. It is as if you come into a restaurant where others eat certain dishes you liked with great appetite while you are on a strict diet and cannot eat them, but you remember how good they once tasted."

25. Young man about his girl friend: "She remains mostly on the surface when we discuss something, but sometimes she gets the bug and then she pushes her feminine point home with perpetual insistence. It wears you out."

26. Young man: "I felt agreeably weakened after sex and when I left her and took a taxi home, I sang 'Oh, what a beautiful morning!'"

27. Psychologist: "I sometimes think that the screaming and loud giggling of girls are only attention-getting devices."

28. Middle-aged man: "I can still remember a time when as a teen-ager I went to movies in which a woman was pursued by a persistent and violent lover and saved her virginity in the last critical moment. Such a performance would today seem to me not to be only unrealistic but also ridiculous. The reverse scene could well be imag-

ined—that a determined woman desperately tries to get
rid of her virginity and the boy gets away at the last moment since he is terrified that he is being tricked and
trapped into marriage."

29. Young man: 'Get out of here,' she cried to me, 'and
never come back! I do not want to see you ever again in
my life!' The next morning early she rang the bell of my
apartment."

30. Young man: ". . . and there I saw a mummy lying
in bed. I assure you, I thought first of an Egyptian
mummy instead of a young American woman whose face
was covered with mud."

"I have to share her with her husband, of course, and I
am not really jealous. But I suspect that she has a compulsion to count, at least to count and to compare the number
of sexual intercourses she has with him and with me."

"It is not difficult to make a girl. What's difficult is to
make an end with her finally. You know, I thought the
other day that the situation is similar to that of a burglar
for whom it is easy to break into a house but who cannot
find his way out later on."

"She is sexually active. She can be persuasive at the
same time. She says, for instance: 'He is not small. He is
growing up. Look how tall he becomes. He will still be a
giant, a Goliath.' "

"I never know what it means when a woman says 'I am
not that kind of a girl.' Are there different kinds of girls?"

"This girl asked me whether I cared for her mind. I was
tempted to answer that I cared more for her behind."

"It is now more than three months since we were together. I feel longings for her in my heart and in my body
even more."

31. A Catholic man: "The Church teaches us to pray:
'Don't lead us into temptation,' but I complain that there

are so few occasions in my life in which I am led into temptation."

32. Middle-aged lawyer: "Women are strange creatures. I still don't understand them. I have been divorced for nine years. My ex-wife has remarried, loves her new husband, and has a child by him. But would you believe it? She is still jealous of my new mistress, whom she does not even know but about whom she says many bad things."

"I had a scene with her. She shouted and cried and behaved melodramatically. I said to her 'Ring down the curtain!' She was very astonished at that and said 'I did not know that any curtain was up.' "

"We had a terrible scene. At the end she said 'Fuck yourself!' and I asked her how this is done. Perhaps she would show me—and better still, I said, let's do it together."

33. Bachelor: "That girl thinks that I shall marry her because I slept with her several times. Why should I marry just her? More than half of the population of the earth are women."

"I believe that there is in the life of every man a sexual experience that he tries to recapture, often in vain."

34. Young man: "I have no high opinion for women's exercises as they are advertised in the magazines. Regular bed-gymnastic is sufficient. You know, pelvis up, legs widely apart and high in the air."

"Women always think an affair must lead to marriage or it must be broken off after a certain time when their hope to be married is not fulfilled."

"Divorce is much easier than breaking with a woman with whom you have had an affair. Some women get very nasty to a man. One went so far that she threatened she would denounce me to the director of Internal Revenue."

"The girl is exceptional. When an argument begins between us, she sometimes uses a weapon that is rare with women. She becomes silent."

"'Leticia,' I said to her, 'you are unique. After God made you, He threw away the mold. We'll never see anyone like you.'"

35. Young man: "I was just now in the pharmacy and saw something called Eyelash trick. It is a recent device in which eyelashes and mascara are provided together. I said to the young druggist 'Oh, women have a thousand tricks,' and he answered 'And not only physical ones.' You're telling me, I thought."

The same young man: "Did you ever observe how women who have had lunch together say good-by to each other? A man says ' 'By!' to his friend and leaves. Women begin to say good-by to each other and rarely end in less than half an hour. They must continue to talk. They are perhaps afraid other people would think they are deaf-mutes if they did not."

"Joan is an angel in her good moods, but when she feels the slightest criticism, she is proud as Lucifer."

About his mistress: "Her first feeling and movement are almost always genuine, but then she gets melodramatic like an actress who plays a part."

36. A patient compared store windows with women. He said that the most attractive and conspicuous things are displayed in both the windows and the appearance of women. "There are, of course, certain objects of inferior value inside the store which are shown to certain customers and not to others, mostly trash. Women have toilette secrets, for instance, falsies they would never show anyone, perhaps not even their best women friends. On the other hand, stores have choice pieces which only a few preferred customers will be allowed to see, and there are parts

of the feminine body which only favored men catch sight
of."

37. Young man discussing women: "The first thing I
appreciate in a young female body is cleanliness. Cleanliness is nearest to goddessliness."

"Listen to two women on a bus. How excitedly they
talk! What gestures they make, and what play of the facial muscles and what animated facial expressions! And
you know what all that excitement was about? I listened.
About the dress of another woman!"

38. Man in his early sixties: "I heard a physician jokingly saying 'When the arteries begin to harden, the penis
begins to get soft.' "

39. Man coming into the room: "I just saw on Broadway a big new store announcing on every window 'Grand
opening' on this or that date. I never saw an advertisement for the 'Grand closing' of a store. It is as with love.
Its beginning is generally proudly and extensively published, but the end of it is mostly hushed up."

40. Young man: "When we came to the pharmacy, she
did not want to go in to buy the pessary and finally asked
me if I could not go in and buy it for her after she told me
the size and kind."

41. Observation of a man on a bus: "The girl sitting
across from me was quite attractive. She read the afternoon newspaper. It disturbed me that she moved her lips
while she read. Only rather uneducated people do this."

42. Man about a certain woman: "She told me all about
her unhappy marriage and it sounded very genuine. Only
later on I recognized that it was a beautiful performance.
She played the part of the neglected wife. She is always
acting and she tells the truth only in an emergency."

43. A young man who knew that a girl with whom

he sometimes slept also occasionally had other sexual partners was nevertheless disturbed by an experience that puzzled him: "Inge phoned me and said she would come over last evening. When she came, she told me she was hot and bothered and expected her period perhaps next day or so. We slept together and she said a few minutes later: 'You are the best of them.' I fell then asleep almost immediately. In the morning she again wanted to have sexual intercourse and stimulated me. I had an erection, but then I suddenly slipped out of her."

During that psychoanalytic session I was able to explain to him that the memory of what Inge had said the evening before must have returned and reminded him that she had had other men with whom she compared him ["You are the best of them"] and this must have disturbed him so that he became impotent. It is obvious that his knowledge of Inge's promiscuity was not present so much before as immediately after the sexual experience when she had made that comparison.

44. "Her everyday language is a sequence of superlatives and I sometimes asked myself how does she speak when she gets alarmed or excited."

"Young girls should only in rare cases go to parties and other social occasions with their mothers. A young man looks at the girl and then at her mother and often thinks that in twenty years she will look exactly like her mother."

45. Young man about an experience of his: "So we slept together. When she and I went to a restaurant later on, she gave me her telephone number. I looked it up in the Manhattan telephone book. I didn't find her name in it and I became suspicious. Coming back to our table, I asked her about it and she then told me that she was married. The telephone number she had given me was

that of her mother, and she told me too at what time she could usually be reached there. Only then did I understand, of course."

46. Older man, a widower: "It's funny. I get old. When I was young, I always attentively looked at pretty waitresses in the restaurants where I had dinner. Now I turn my attention more and more to the dishes they are serving."

47. Man whose wife does not want to give him a divorce to marry another woman: "If she loves me as she says, would she not wish me to be happy with someone else?"

48. Bachelor: "I cannot afford to go away this summer. I am thirty-two years old and New York is the greatest city of the world. Where else could I run into a very nice Jewish girl?"

After a sexual adventure: "What are all those pretenses for? To hell with face and figure! The penis has its own requirements and even a plain woman can meet them, if she is passionate enough."

"Some women are sexually in such a deep freeze that it takes a long time to thaw them and a small eternity until you can make them melt."

Telling about his summer: "I said to her 'Don't you think that a straw hat with a wide brim would protect you even better against the sun? It would be very becoming too. If one has as beautiful eyes as you, one should not wear dark sunglasses. Beauty obliges.'"

About his friend: "He is always afraid that he will not live up to the image his wife made of him. I mean that he does not come up to the sexual expectations she then had."

49. Misogynistic patient: "In these summer days women are on the streets in lofty dresses. It is a vanity fair of the revealed and hidden flesh. They are all show-offs even

when they conceal what they have to offer. All women hope that we men will guess that there is more than meets the eye. It is often much less. . . ."

"I drove a long time beside a car in which there was a lady driver and another woman. They were in animated conversation. I could, of course, not hear what they were saying, but I observed their very eloquent gestures and their changing facial expressions. It was as if seeing people dancing in the distance without hearing the music."

50. Another patient shows a friendlier attitude: "I was just sitting in Central Park for a while. You know women are really much more broadly democratic then we men. There was a New England lady chatting with a Negress about children and later on she talked about dresses with a Jewish girl. Yes, women are charitably democratic. . . . And think how patient they can be! A woman with packages ascends a bus and sits comfortably down. Only then does she take out the fare for the driver. They are not so punctual nor so painfully exact as we men, more lenient and lax. They don't give a damn about regulations and rules when it is inconvenient, while we stupid men are often atrociously priggish and adhere to fixed principles."

"Jeanne loves me, I know, but, alas, she is allergic to sexuality."

51. Married man whose wife had suffered from incurable schizophrenia for several years and is in a mental hospital: "When I now sometimes think of her, I still love her, but I love her as a phantom. I see her as she was—young, beautiful, and vivid—when I met her and fell in love with her."

52. A young man speaking of a sexual scene with a college girl: "That Lisa is like a child. Whatever you give her, she takes into her mouth."

53. Patient, about his girl friend: "Sure, she is faithful.

The only trouble is that she is faithful to me today and faithful to another man tomorrow."

The same young man: "When I see a woman who is not blindly hurrying and who is not dangerously ill passing by a mirror without looking at herself, I become suspicious. I then think it could be a transvestite man."

"I saw that young girl. She was alone and I went over to her. I thought 'She is a sitting duck.' I later found out that she was rather a sitting goose."

"You know the nicest noise in the streets of New York? The clack of high heels behind you."

"To cover up her embarrassment, Anne became quite impudent and impertinent and attacked me. She reproached me for all."

"I really believe that women see more than they hear. Take, for instance, Anne. When I talk about the situation on the stock exchange, or about politics, or something serious, she listens with half an ear, *sans dire mot.* But she looks at me very attentively. She examines me with her eyes and I sometimes anticipate that she will say 'There is some dandruff on your collar.'

"The thought that one must die drives everybody into a sexual orgy as if this would be an escape route. It's funny that after sexual intercourse the thought of death reemerges: *Omne animal triste.* When I walk around in the park late in the evenings, the love couples there remind me of a *danse macabre,* of those medieval presentations of the death-dance."

"There are good and bad lays, but Eileen, the wife of the architect, was the greatest. I remember that she took me into her bedroom while her husband had a nap in the neighboring room. She stood against the door from where he could have come any minute, lifted her skirt—she had nothing on underneath—and took me into her. It was the most perfect orgasm I experienced."

About another woman: "I turned her over and tried to enter her from behind, you know. I liked it better. It was easier and she was lubricating."

Other remarks of the same young man about other sexual experiences: "'Are you already going?' she said when she opened her eyes afterward. It was a bedroom-cliché whether I left after an hour or after two days."

"She must have felt that I was getting tired of her because she sometimes asked me about sex. 'What do you like? Tell me what I should do to you? How do you like sex?' But I was not only tired of her sexually, but of her love too."

"I was then hard up—I mean in sex—or should I say I had always a hard one?"

"After I kissed her mouth many times, I descended to lower altitudes, to her breasts and to her navel and even lower than this."

54. Another young man, more philosophically inclined than the preceding one: "Adam had it easy. There was Eve and no one else to pay attention to. He could take her or leave her as he felt at a certain moment."

"Polonius sent those precepts to Laertes. He could not have sent them to Ophelia, nor to any other woman: 'This above all: to thine own self be true.' No woman knows what her own self is and none would want to be true to it."

55. Graduate student, working on his thesis in English literature, speaks about his sexual experiences: "Some memories come back when you least expect them. The other day I looked something up in the variorum edition of *Hamlet* and opened the book at the play scene. You

remember, of course, that the prince there makes a few bawdy allusions. Ophelia tells him: 'You are keen, my lord, you are keen' and Hamlet answers: 'It could cast you a groaning to take off my edge.' The sexual allusion, but especially the word *groaning* triggered off the memory of a scene I vividly re-experienced. We were in bed and Eileen was sitting straddling me with her face toward the other side; I only stroked her behind. She by and by became aroused and made the to-and-fro movement of a desperately wild rider. She really groaned until she felt my ejaculation within her, until she took off my edge."

56. Young man: "I do not believe that those pornographic inscriptions and drawings to be found on the walls of our streets and in toilets could ever be made by women. They are really sexual attacks on women by way of words and pictures."

57. Producer: "Women are excellent stage managers of their own plays. This means when they play themselves, so to speak, their own part. I do not think that they are so good in plays written by others."

58. Young man: "Sometimes a passing skirt can arouse me more than a naked woman."

59. Young man about his mistress: "Cecily likes to do it rather on the floor than in the bed and rather in the woods than in a room. She says she is a primitive . . . At first she said: 'Come into me!' but later on she avoided such euphemisms and said: 'Fuck me!' She also asked me to use four-letter words such as *fuck* and *cunt*. It was if she wanted to be degraded. . . .

"I remember the first time when she took the initiative. She then said jokingly she liked to explore unknown countries and opened my fly. She knew quite well what she would find there. But she liked to feel in her fingers how it would grow and become hard."

The same young man: "It's not the dresses, but the choice of her underwear that decides whether a woman is really feminine or not."

60. Man recollecting his college years: "Then I went with the gang to a brothel. I had to borrow money from one of the fellows. I did not know then that the best things in life are free, otherwise I would not have gone with the guys."

61. *The opinions of a young man about women:* What now follows is a collection of sayings from psychoanalytic sessions during two years of treatment. The patient, a man in his early thirties, speaks about various women and himself, speaks of his adventures and insights. With his marriage a certain phase of his life entered a more satisfactory period.

About an insignificant sexual experience: "It was really not much. *Les petits riens* so to speak, or rather *Eine kleine Nachtmusik*—only it was not so beautiful. . . . When I was young, I was much more timid with women. You live and learn. I learned especially which are the best tactics to follow with them when you want to conquer them. The whole secret is: Be gentle at first and then bold. When a certain point is reached, a point of no return, you must go ahead without concern for your sexual partner. Only in this way do you secure the greatest pleasure for her and for yourself. . . . When a woman allows you to gently stroke her nipples and you continue this for a long time, you can bet that she will finally grasp your penis. It is almost automatic. . . . Sometimes sexual intercourse is not worth the effort. The French have a saying: *Le jeu ne vaut pas la chandelle.* That means the play is not worth the candles you light for it. In this particular case it is not worth the candle you sometimes extinguish before your start. . . . [In a philosophical mood] The sexual desire does not only make strange bed-fellows, but also bedfellows who remain strangers to each other in spite of the common sexual experience. But that experience is sometimes not common, but one-sided and sometimes scarcely that. . . . [About a certain girl] The next time we met was at a dinner party where she was my neighbor. She was unnaturally natural about the night we had spent together the previous week.

[About himself] I must make compromises, for in-stance, sleeping with a woman I really don't like. These are mostly measures dictated by emergency. You know, one could compare such situations with the umbrellas that butlers and hotel-doorkeepers put up when they take guests from the car to the house when there is heavy rain or a snowstorm. It helps for the moment. . . . . Some-times you have no longing for this or that girl. You just want a woman, any woman. . . . [About a certain girl] Anne? It would need a Shakespearean fantasy to im-agine that one could go to bed with her. The very thought could make you impotent—not to mention the deed. . . . [About another woman] No, I did not yet make great progress with her. It is as if you were still on the runway, moving, but you already know that in a short time the plane will be in the air. . . . [Speaking of still another woman] She is a snake in the grass and I sometimes feel in her presence like a snake-charmer who has left his flute at home. . . . "Good-by!" I said to her before I got into the plane. "Good-bye and more power to you!" But later on I thought "God forbid that she should get more power over me." . . . Women are so curious about details. You tell them you had an argument in the office and they want to know with whom and what was it about and how it went. And when you mention that the boss' wife came to the office to pick him up, they ask how she greeted him and what he said to her and want you to describe how she was dressed. . . .

[After his marriage] Yesterday after dinner my wife asked me to tell her about my experiences with girls before I met her or rather before I married her. She wanted to know all the details about them and what was my relationship to each of them and all that. I told her that she has to wait until I write my memoirs under the title *My Life and Loves.* . . . I had a row with my wife. Afterward in the late evening I went up to Jane and slept with her not because I wanted to, but because I wanted to take revenge on my wife.

2 Man and marriage

1. Marriage seems to arouse more misgivings and grievances in men than in women—quite apart from the money question, where the man fills the traditional role of breadwinner. The complaint of a patient may serve as a kind of prelude: "First it was misery from which I tried to escape into marriage, then it was marriage with misery. . . . You know, they lived unhappily ever afterwards. . . ." Yet the same patient reported that he had often been warned by a much older man who told him: "Be always ready to be best man at the weddings of your friends, but be never the bridegroom!"—quite in contrast to the often-quoted complaint of the girls: "Always the bridesmaid, never the bride."

If marriage were so intolerable to men as they sometimes assert, how can it be explained that the majority of them remain married? I once heard an older man describe the behavior of a younger: "It's always the same with him. He falls in love with some girl, wants to divorce his wife and marry that girl, and he almost does. But it is always *almost*. At the last moment he throws the girl over and returns to his wife and children."

There is, of course, the case of the eternal bachelor, one of whom declared to me: "No, I am not the marrying kind. I am the screwing type."

2. A lawyer describes a courtroom scene in an injury case: "Then the husband of the woman, who was still in the hospital, was called to testify. He said that he did all the household chores which his wife had performed prior to her accident. In cross-examination the witness was asked how much time he was spending in the household tasks, and he answered 'Woman's work is never done.' The jurors laughed and even the judge smiled."

3. A middle-aged man declared: "I do not believe what the statisticians declare, that married men live longer than bachelors. It only appears longer when you are married."

4. Bachelors sometimes experience a kind of desire for family life. One said: "I am getting old; I'll be thirty-two shortly. I became aware of my age yesterday. I stood before the window of Schwartz—you know, the toy store on Fifth Avenue—and a mother with her little boy stood beside me. The child pointed out various things in the show window to his mother. She smiled at him and I smiled too. By God, I wanted to go into the store and buy something for the boy. When I walked along I suddenly thought that I am an old bachelor and I felt depressed at the thought that I could be one of the people who leave their money to an orphanage."

5. "Whatever the tiff is about, my wife has always the last word. Did you read the story of that Irishman who asserted that his wife has the last word even to the echo?"

"There are unquestionable facts, things she and I have seen, but she sometimes denies them with the most passionate and indignant protest."

6. A patient talking about the past: "I know she was not very pretty and not well educated, but I had only debts and I decided to marry her. 'Beggars cannot be choosers.' Money does not grow on trees, but it came from her father's lumber mills."

7. Let us now listen to the various griefs and grievances a psychoanalyst hears his married patients recount: "My wife spends a lot of money on cosmetics and makeup in order to look natural. . . . The other day we had an argument about it. You know what she said at the end of it? 'A woman, right or wrong, is always right.'"

"My wife makes me responsible for all that is wrong. I think she accuses me of having started the second world war."

"After that argument my wife, the bitch, put me into the doghouse for two weeks."

"When one is married for a long time, one learns that sexual intercourse and pleasure are sometimes very different things and should not be confused. People very correctly speak of sexual intercourse in marriage as conjugal duty. It is often only that."

"Genesis says that from Chaos comes order. My wife is fanatic about order and as merciless about it as Jehovah. When she puts things in order on my desk, my notes and my manuscripts, I need a long time to find them."

"We had that tiff yesterday. My wife said: 'Good, you will have your way, but I will have my say' and then she began to talk and talk. Her say had not yet finished when I left the house today."

"Yesterday my wife was in her mink mood. That means the mood when she tries by hook and by crook to bring me so far that I buy her a mink coat. Finally I decided to buy her the coat. She need not know that it will be imitation mink, of course."

"I never heard my wife say 'I am now ready' when we go out. She always says 'I am not yet dressed' or 'I have not finished.' "

"My wife is funny. On the days when the maid comes in to clean the apartment, she gets up very early in the morning and works like a coolie for many hours. She works hard so that the maid will find the apartment in excellent condition, in perfect order, and spotlessly clean when she arrives to clean the rooms."

"I told my wife she must not think so much. First because the result is not worth the effort. Nothing is decided in women's thoughts anyhow, since they make their decisions according to their emotional condition. Secondly, brooding makes them knit their brows. Which thought of a woman is worth such a wrinkled forehead? Thirdly, her thinking is expensive—since I as the husband have to pay Helena Rubinstein for removing those wrinkles."

"My wife never convinces me, of course, because I know all she has to say is nonsense, but she sometimes persuades me although I never listen to what she says, only to the modulation of her voice."

Man in his sixties: "I caught my wife when she searched my shirt for lipstick traces and I said to her 'Your suspicions flatter me very much. I wish they could have been justified.' "

"My wife is terribly jealous. We were in a movie yesterday and I expressed my admiration for Marilyn Monroe several times. My wife became so jealous that she kicked my leg whenever I said something about the beauty of

Monroe. I did not know her, of course, and besides she is dead."

"My wife cannot be punctual: I at first thought that this was a congenital handicap, but then she once came on time. She thought she had been invited an hour earlier."

Patient talking about his summer vacations: "In the hotel was a table next to mine at which a woman and a man sat during these weeks. They never talked together and I thought that they either did not know each other or that they were married for many years."

"Women have in general a greater respect for public opinion, for what people think or say of them, than men. My wife tells me that she does not care what people think of her. Only what they say."

"My wife spends a lot of time on makeup. I once heard a woman say *'Je fais ma tête.'* Women usurp the place of God. When they are not satisfied with the face He has given them they fabricate another one. It is rarely an improvement."

Middle-aged man: "My wife is funny. When I do not work and rest on the couch, she says, 'Why don't you work? You don't talk to me and you don't show the slightest interest in me anyhow. Should you not work?' When I am working she says: 'There, you are reading and writing and you do not pay any attention to me, only to your work.' "

Man in his forties: "Life with my wife—I mean my married life—is rocky. You understand, everything is pleasant

—plenty of surface, but no content to that life. A few years ago I was still hammering against the walls of married life as if it were a prison. But there was no exit. My wife and my children had jailed me. And then I met Debbie and had that sexual experience that I still treasure. It was as if those walls were slowly melting away."

"My wife sometimes stands so long before the mirror that I often imagine she will go through the looking-glass as Alice did."

"My wife nags me and shows me again and again that I am careless about putting cigarette ashes into the ash-trays. I told her today: 'You have missed your profession. You should have become a governess.' Some women behave like governesses toward their husbands as well as toward all other men."

Man in his fifties: "I am against love matches. A French writer—I don't now remember his name—once called love *une promesse du bonheur.* I have seen many couples who married for love. In most cases love was rather *une promesse du malheur.* Two people in love—that means two people who have many misconceptions about each other."

Seventy-two-year-old man in consultation: "My wife tries to reform me, to make me give up my bad habits, but one cannot do that to an old fellow like me. I read the other day that Talleyrand said '*C'est plus qu'un crime, c'est une stupidité.*' . . . Whenever I smoke a cigarette, she is there to empty the ashtray. I tell her: 'Don't go away, stand by; in a few seconds I shall again flick the ashes.'"

X Miscellany

The fifth part of this book has a character different from that of the preceding ones, each of which had a definite and unified content. The first part presented the history of the volume's genesis. The second part was devoted to the views and sayings of women about each other, about men, and so on. Those views are not only spoken, but often outspoken and sometimes outpoured, as is possible only in psychoanalytic sessions. The third and fourth parts are filled with the words of male patients, who expressed their opinions in a quite uninhibited manner.

The four preceding parts, then, present many witty and perceptive things patients have said during their sessions. Some of them will have amused and some may have amazed the reader, but in the following part he may learn new things which will lead to new insights.

I consider this fifth section the most important of the book. It contains memories of Freud not before published, and findings and case histories presented by psychoanalysts and their students in lectures and seminars, as well as my own contributions. I trust that this miscellany will answer a few questions, whet the thirst for knowledge, and appeal to the interest in human concerns which we all feel. I hope furthermore that some of the following contributions (for instance, the memories of Freud) will be endearing and that some of the psychoanalytic insights may be enduring.

1. A writer: "I cannot show the first draft or part of an unfinished manuscript. It would be as if you received a visitor while not yet washed and still in your underwear."

2. Thoughtful woman: "If love were only a parlor game, we women would have an easy victory; but it is also a bedroom game. It's there we often lose and there we sometimes become hopeless."

3. "Never underestimate the power of a woman" could never have been said or written by a woman. A woman exercises her power, but never talks about it to men. The slogan could not have originated with a he-man because he does not think woman has any power and does not surmise by what devious ways she leads him where not he, but she, wants him to go. The best conjecture is that that sentence was originally said or written by a fairly intelligent man who did just that—underestimate the power of a woman—and had a rather trying experience. The sentence sounds more like the sudden insight of a man who had been unexpectedly hurt than like an objective statement.

4. *On the psychology of lesbianism.* The emotional preconditions of female homosexuality are difficult to understand so long as one does not differentiate the two main types of lesbian fantasy. In one type, the couple imagines and play-acts being mother and child; one partner treats the other as a mother treats her girl child. In the other type, the two women play-act, so to speak, man and woman, and the roles can sometimes be exchanged. In both cases a real or imagined early disappointment of love or a denial of affection is one of the emotional motives for the fantasy in which the part of mother or lover has been appropriated by one of the principals.

5. *Origin of repression.* We pay too little attention to the fact that the dynamic processes with which psychoanalysis copes, such as repression, denial, and disavowal, originally come from outside the individual. Parents, teachers, and others induce children to restrain their impulses. Later on, inner agencies take over the part of those educators and continue their work—not always successfully.

Paradise lost was not childhood, which is often full of conflicts, but the situation of the embryo within the uterus, the intrauterine situation. Birth already marks the expulsion from that paradise into rough life. When we fall asleep, we are attempting to regain that lost paradise. We shut out the external world and its stimuli and we try to restore the conditions of the embryo within the uterus: darkness, warmth, and self-sufficiency.

6. *A technical contribution to psychoanalysis* was made in a seminar-discussion. As is well known, longer pauses and silences of the patient in analytic sessions indicate that he is consciously or unconsciously suppressing something unpleasant to express, often a critical comment on or a hostile impulse toward the analyst. In such situations the analyst will—especially at the beginning of treatment—sometimes help the patient express his resistances. The seminar-discussion centered around the direct form of such help. An analyst in the described situation asked the patient: "Did you just now not think anything critical about me?" We agreed that it would be preferable to put the question into a more general form, for instance: "Did anything occur to you concerning me?"

7. *In the dream of a patient,* striped globes, traditional in front of barber shops, appeared. In his thought-associations the patient remembered that he had felt as a small child intense anxiety whenever he saw those stripes on a barber pole. He experienced the same emotion in his

dream. The nature of that anxiety, as well as that part of the dream in which it emerged, remained puzzling. In another context the patient remembered that his father had taken him several times to the barber for haircuts when he was small. As happens so often with male children, he connected the barber, the scissors, and the process of haircutting with castration. He was therefore afraid of barbers and experienced a kind of phobia when he saw the stripes before their shops.

8. A patient, a young woman inclined to promiscuity: "When I dressed for the party yesterday, I caught myself in the thought 'I should take that new black underwear. You never know what kind of attractive young men you will run into at these parties.'" On another occasion: "When he opened the door for me, the vestibule was dark; he turned the light on and said: 'Let me look at you!'" I don't know why, but I suddenly thought of Little Red Riding Hood and of the Wolf who told her 'Better to see you with.' Oh yes, he is a wolf."

9. My own case: "I never learned to drive a car and I am never nervous in a car whoever drives it—except when one of my two daughters is at the wheel. They are both in their twenties and are reliable and experienced drivers. When one of them takes the car and I am in it, I never tire of admonishing them: 'Be careful!' 'Here comes a car!' 'Slowly now!' and so on. The explanation for this behavior is simple: While I consciously know that they are adults, I unconsciously consider my daughters little girls who are, of course, unable to drive a car."

10. Married man: "I heard a nice little story the other day. A woman says to her husband at breakfast: 'I dreamed that you gave me a mink stole!' 'You may keep it,' says the husband." Not all husbands are so generous as the one in this anecdote.

11. A psychoanalyst provided an interesting dream interpretation in a seminar. The patient introduced his report saying: "I had a dream last night and it frightened me: I was in the old apartment where we lived when I was a little boy, perhaps five years old. In the dream I was lying in bed with my face pressed to the pillow. Someone came in, I believe it was my sister Jean. I was absolutely frozen with fear and could not move. I could not see anything."

The patient had in the analytic session the day before spoken of his childhood memories and had remembered that he had shared a bedroom with his older sister until he was past five years old. The psychoanalyst used these day-remnants reconstructing the latent dream content. The dream can be understood when its manifest content is reversed. The little boy must have observed his sister undressing and felt intense castration fear because he saw no penis. (Governed by the boy's belief that the penis could also be taken from him.) While the dream distortion is reached by the reversal (pressed against the pillow . . . could not see anything), the vivid emotion of fear is preserved and experienced.

12. A patient: "Jean and I had a date for yesterday evening, but she did not turn up. She perhaps confused the place; I waited in vain. Finally I missed the bus home. That's good, isn't it? Did you not tell me that buses and cars are symbolically representative of women in dreams?"

13. *General Observation.* An expert is usually a man who has arrived at a great deal of knowledge and insights progressing from more errors of judgment, trials, and mistakes than the other people who imagine they know all about a special field.

14. Patient about a couple: "It's a strange marriage. His wife knows, of course, about his homosexual adventures.

There is no doubt about who wears the panties in this family."

15. *Psychoanalysis.* Here is a psychological observation that has never been met with in psychoanalytic literature on the technique in practice. When the analyst wants to penetrate the latent meaning of a dream or understand the unconscious sense of a symptom, he must withdraw his attention from the area of clear conscious thought. That means he must neglect the region of conscious mind before he can descend into the mental nether world and become aware of the processes there. A comparison will illustrate what I mean: When you turn off the electric light in your room and then try while your eyes are open to recognize the objects in the room, you will fail. Their outlines become recognizable only after you shut your eyes for a few seconds and then open them. This kind of adaptation is necessary before you begin to understand the meaning of unconscious processes within the patient and yourself. The device valid for the process is expressed in Goethe's *Torquato Tasso*

> *Und lass dir sagen, habe die Sonne*
> *Nicht zu lieb und nicht die Sterne,*
> *Komm, folge mir ins dunkle Reich hinab.*

> [And let me tell you: don't like
>   the sun too much, nor the stars.
> Come, follow me down into the
>   dark country.]

16. *Mock modesty:* Our narcissism reaches much further down than we guess. It reaches so far that it approaches self-deification. I read the other day an anecdote about General de Gaulle which makes fun of him, but reminded me of that unconscious core of narcissism in everyone.

After the last elections a partisan came to De Gaulle and said: "My God, you were again victorious!" De Gaulle replied: *"Merci bien,* but please call me *Mon General!"*

17. *Sexuality and morality:* In morals there is the valid sentence "What you do not want done to you don't inflict on another person." The sexual foreplay is characterized by the sentence "What you want to be done to you, do to the other"—certain caresses you confer on your partner indicate to him or her what he should do to you.

18. *Familiarity:* When a woman has lost a certain mysterious quality for a man, as after a long married life, she has lost something very valuable that can only rarely be regained. Familiarity in this case breeds not contempt but sexual indifference.

19. *Conversation:* A woman says: "Female conversations are but rarely as stimulating as men's—not even to men, except perhaps sexually stimulating."

20. *Impressions:* When you return from a long absence to a city in which you lived many years, you have the impression that you know or have at least seen many persons you encounter on the streets, buses, and so on. This impression decreases in intensity after many days spent in this old-new surrounding.

21. A writer about a critic who published a review of a novel: "This critic is highly intelligent but he does not understand the psychology of the writer. He does not understand that a writer does not choose his subject, but is chosen by it. It is an experience beyond the writer's choice just as, for instance, falling in love."

About another writer: "You know, after he had published his book, his publicity agent threw him to the lions and the lion-hunters."

22. A man about a conversation with another man the day before: "I gave him that as a thought for the day. It

occurred to me that this is enough for him and perhaps even too much."

23. A patient spoke of another woman whose mother did not react favorably to a suggestion by the daughter that she visit the mother who lived several hundred miles away. The mother finally answered evasively in a letter in which she mentioned her heart condition. The patient telling me about this asked: "Can you imagine that? It is a real Anglo-Saxon attitude. A Jewish woman would have said, with her last breath, 'Come!'"

24. A woman secretary: "My previous boss was straightforward, and when he did not like something he said so. The present one is very considerate, but often he becomes devious in order not to hurt people's feelings. We sense that, of course, and sometimes feel much more hurt than otherwise."

25. From a lecture in a seminar: "Gallantry was defined by a dictionary as 'excessive attention to women without serious purpose.' It has a characteristic feature that remained undiscovered. I mean the psychological trait that it is characterized by a small or great self-sacrifice or personal renunciation in favor of the woman. Examples: You let the woman enter a room before you. This means you have to wait and not go ahead. You get up from your chair when a woman enters the room. You thus renounce the comfort of sitting. In most cases the core of that renunciation is simply a waiting, but on many occasions it is more. For instance when you help a woman to put on her overcoat. Here is a small service, a little work done for the woman."

26. Straight posture aids the impression of pride and self-sufficiency women like to give to men. Sitting and walking hunched up is not only unbecoming; it also gives the impression of dependence.

27. *Normal fetishism:* When one wants the measure of normal fetishism* among the males in a big city, it is advantageous to observe how many women wear high-heeled shoes, because the high heels reassure the men who unconsciously experience castration-anxiety (see Freud's paper on fetishism).

28. *Worldly wisdom in simplest terms:* When it is very hot, walk on the shadowy side of the street. When it is very cold, walk on its sunny side.

29. A man about others in his office: "The Jews among them are warm and sometimes even helpful. They are all so unsuspicious about our attitude to them."

30. A stockbroker about a client: "I don't know much about him except that he invests a great deal in certain bonds, but I believe that he is a professional anti-Semite."

31. Another man: "You know, I am not religious. I do not believe in God, but I am a good Jew. Being a Jew, one need not believe in God. Every Jew hears in himself the silent call of humanity which is at the core of religion."

32. "Every one of us knows that he cannot live for ever. If he could, he would perhaps curse this fate. Think of Ahasuerus who could not die and had to wander from land to land as we Jews all must do."

33. Man about his office boss: "He is an amazing combination of arrogance and ignorance."

34. Childhood memory of a man: "When we children entered our aunt's house, she shouted: 'Look what the cat just dragged in.'"

35. Hungarian refugee: "My grandfather was a very pious man and when I was a boy, he often told me fables from the Talmud. I still remember that he told me a child is born with clenched fists as if he wants to grasp the whole

* See my paper "On Universal Fetishism" in *The Need To Be Loved,* New York, 1963, pp. 169ff.

world and an old man dies with his fingers opened: 'The world was nothing.' "

36. Young woman who is compulsively promiscuous, speaking about her latest adventure with a man: "I know I destroyed all my chances since I went to bed with him on our second date." Turning to the psychiatrist, "But what should I have done? Should I have phoned you and asked for your help at one o'clock in the morning?"

37. After the assassination of President John F. Kennedy several women showed a strange kind of mourning that seemed not to be connected with the President's dying. In two cases of this kind the analyst found that the mourning concerned the death of an older brother when the women had still been little girls. In one case the brother died in the war, in the other in an accident. The little girls knew, of course, then that their brothers had been killed, but had scarcely any strong reactions. In the displacement to the President, who was at forty-six a few years older than the women, a very delayed and late mourning found its expression.

38. A young girl living with her widowed mother and grandmother, speaking of the frequent arguments between the two women: "They are lovers' quarrels."

39. Internist, professor at a clinic: "When one gets old, the opinions of the students about oneself become more important than what our patients think of us."

40. A patient told me that he is unable to fall asleep when his hands are underneath the blankets. He himself traces this back to his childhood and to his mother's admonitions to have his hands always away from the penis. His hands are now usually near his head when he sleeps.

41. Patient, interested in semantics: "Do you know that language seems to confirm the psychoanalytic theory of the analerotic character? Especially the connection be-

tween parsimony or avariciousness and constipation. The word *close* has also the connotation of stingy."

42. A man who knows many women asserted that women who don't consider themselves beautiful or pretty always feel attracted to especially handsome men, while most women convinced of their own attractiveness are less concerned about the appearance of the man.

The same man observed during another psychoanalytic session: "Neither Luther's religious zeal nor any other minister's ambition approaches the intensity of determination of a woman who has decided that she will reform a certain man."

43. Woman in her late forties: "As a little girl I was often afraid to leave the house. I would not go to kindergarten and I made terrible scenes when I had to go to school. I often had a fantasy that an earthquake could come and make an abyss in the middle of the room so that my mother and father and myself would be separated from each other. Only many years later when I was in psychoanalysis it dawned on me what that childhood fantasy really meant. There was a terrible conflict between my parents when I was a little girl and I was always afraid that they would be separated—I perhaps wished it. At the same time, I feared that there would be a great scene at home when I was in school or away from the house and I was terrified at the thought that I would find my parents and myself separated from each other when I returned from school. The earthquake is only the visual expression of those fears. I had perhaps seen pictures of earthquakes in the magazines then."

44. A middle-aged Irishwoman: "You know, I have that fighting spirit from my parents and from their parents. We Irish all have it. My father once told me a story about an Irishman who walked on the street late in the evening and

happened to see two groups of men in a violent scuffle. He asked: 'Is this a private fight or is it a free-for-all?' "

45. This description by a patient presents a good picture of an obsessional thought-process: "You know my mind always works with suspenseful delay. There are only fleeting thoughts, but they have the character of strict orders from within. For instance: I walk out from my apartment to the elevator and feel like lighting a cigarette. Then it occurs to me: Begin to smoke only after you have left the house. I must then wait until the elevator comes up and takes me down. Then the steps down in the hall and out. Only then do I allow myself to smoke. The same prohibition I experience, for instance, at breakfast when I have a hard-boiled egg. I like the yolk best, but I have to postpone eating it until I have consciously eaten every bit of the white. Since the suspense gets more and more prolonged in my thoughts, where can this lead to? Only in a voluntary or rather unvoluntary renunciation of gratification, of denying myself every pleasure—perhaps even in sex. . . . It is possible that I'll end as a rigid ascetic."

46. A man who reads a lot of fiction: "The majority of women do not like mystery stories, especially those in which murders are committed. I understand that, because the description of murder and violence repels women. What I don't understand is that some of our best mystery stories are written by women, Agatha Christie and others. I would like to meet and to know some of those female mystery-story writers. Perhaps they have intensive masculine traits."

47. A patient: "I walked on Broadway last evening and felt depressed and lonely. No girl, no friend, no relative. On the corner of Seventy-second Street I read an announcement in big letters on the walls of a house. It

said YOU HAVE A FRIEND AT THE CHASE MANHATTAN BANK. Well, I thought, I have at least one friend!"

48. A sociologist says: "Women are temperamentally conformists. They have a natural strong herd instinct—except in regard to their dresses, hats, and so on, by which each wants to be an individual, not to be confused with any other woman."

"People who have the same emotional conflict or suffer from the same physical illness should not be thrown together. There is, of course, at first some interest in comparing oneself with the others, but then later they bore each other to tears."

49. One of my most gifted students, who is a good teacher and speaker, has difficulties when he wants to write down his often brilliant ideas. When someone suggested that he could perhaps make it easier for himself if he would use the dictaphone, he said: "I cannot relate to a machine."

50. A patient in his first thought associations: "I just saw in a store on Broadway a board on which was printed NACHERY DEPARTMENT. Isn't it odd that so many Jewish-German expressions have now entered into New York language? *Naschen*—it is differently spelled in German—means to eat on the sly, also to enjoy forbidden food. The Viennese said 'naschen' for taking dainty bits or delicacies. *Nachery* is a funny mixture of Viennese, Jewish, and English."

51. A student treating his first psychoanalytic case in self-criticism: "The patient in the middle of his thought association began suddenly to sing a church hymn. I told him that this was a maneuver of diversion. I now think that this was a mistake. I should have paid attention to the text of that hymn."

The same student, a year later: "I asked the patient

whether he was aware that during the whole year of psychoanalytic treatment he never had said anything friendly or grateful to me, and he said: 'If I wanted to say something nice to you, I would have to hit you first.' "

52. *Childhood memory:* "My mother once took me to father's office. I was then a little boy and I was very much impressed by the many pencils and pens he had on his desk. They appeared to me then, I am sure, as expressions of his omnipotence."

Another childhood memory, told me by a woman whose father was taken by the Nazis to a concentration camp in Poland when she was five years old: "I thought then that he went away because I had been a naughty little girl and I felt very guilty about it. I always hoped he would return home if I would be a good and obedient child."

53. Young man: "Perfume on a woman disturbs and distracts me. I read the other day that the famous Point, who was one of the great representatives of *la grande cuisine* in France, did not permit flowers on the tables during meals because their scent distracted from the flavor of the dishes. In the same way I like women who have their natural female scent."

54. Jewish man speaking of an argument he had had the day before: "He called me a son of a gun. I am nothing of the kind. I never shot a gun in my life. I never understood the pleasure some people have in hunting. I know it would not be a pleasure for me. I once read in Heinrich Heine's writings that he did not feel like hunting because his ancestors belonged rather to the hunted than to the hunters."

55. Man in his sixties: "As long as you are young, you want to scrape together as much money as you can. Now I am rich, and what do I do with the money I have? I worry about whether I should divide it among my children

and grandchildren in such a way that none of them feels wronged. First scraping it all up and then distributing— does that make sense?"

56. Obese young man: "Yesterday I was at my doctor's. He weighed me and gave me, finally, the advice: 'Chew more and eat less.' If I understand you properly, you will now advise me: 'Love more and hate less.'"

57. Jewish woman: "When the Nazis came, I did not need much preparation to leave Austria. I had already led a suitcase existence long before that."

58. Man telling his story: "That old man gave me valuable advice and helped me much when I first came to the Company. I treated him coldly, often felt guilty about it when he suddenly died. It was not arrogance but timidity that made me so ungrateful and unresponsive to his friendliness."

59. A psychiatrist said that he had observed interesting emotional reactions: "It is enough to remark that a woman is not very feminine or a man not very masculine to fill them with terror. It almost sounds to them as if you had said that they are scarcely human beings."

60. An interesting slip of the tongue occurred to a patient who said to his psychiatrist: "Yesterday I thought about how long you had already been a psychopath— pardon me, a psycho*analyst* I wanted to say, of course."

The same patient on another occasion: "I believe that psychoanalysts have impotence as their occupational disease. You know, those who can, do, and those who can't teach."

61. A philosophically inclined patient says: "I don't give a damn about love of mankind. I believe that such a phrase conceals the inability of a person to love his wife, his children, his parents."

. . . "I brought you some lines that Thomas Jefferson

wrote in the last year of his Presidency. I jotted them down for you to think over: 'I wish,' Jefferson wrote, 'that not only no act, but no thought of mine should be unknown.' That was a long time before psychoanalysis, wasn't it?"

62. Lecturer at a university: "I seriously believe that the female fashion of shorts and pants as well as the preference for flat-chested women in our society shows an increase of latent homosexuality."

In a polemic against psychoanalysis: "You analysts do not see how difficult it is to become the person one really is. It even requires a long time to acknowledge what you always somehow knew."

About a scientific project of his: "To have an original idea is like knowing that there is a hidden treasure at a certain place buried in the earth. You must dig and dig until you penetrate and reach it. Or it is like knowing that there is oil in a certain region. If often takes months until you find it at a definite spot."

63. *Additions to Freud's theories:* Freud was a giant who heaped huge rocks at the place where he wished to build the house of his theories. It remains to us, his students, to put those sometimes rough-hewn stones together, to connect them with each other and as often as possible to mix the cement and to apply the mortar.

These excerpts from lecturers in a student's seminar will serve such a purpose. I found only clues for them among the notes in my folder and I make an attempt to reconstruct them here. The man I see in the mirror is not satisfied with this attempt, but it is the best I can do at present.

The first remarks concern the taboo between the sexes and thus form a much-needed complement to the contributions Freud made to that subject in his book *Totem and Taboo* (1915). Let me begin with a relatively late saying. The Book of Proverbs warns "Give not thy strength to women!" There is no doubt that the wise Solomon, son of David and King of Israel, meant this originally in a literal sense and thought that sexual intercourse weakens the male. Beside and beyond this primary consideration is, of course, the other meaning that sexual occupation with women turns the energy away from more important tasks in life. Freud himself, pointing to the numerous instances of periodic sexual abstinence among savage tribes cited by Frazer, states that those sexual restrictions are imposed when the men go hunting or to war. He says the hygienic roots of the forbidding must be considered in addition to all magical rationalizations. He even asserts that the fundamental idea among those savages is to acquire more strength through renouncing satisfaction of the sexual drive.

At this point we return to the sentence from Proverbs and to its first interpretation. In following the economical point of view to which Freud alludes, one reaches the conclusion that sexual indulgence weakens the man—so clearly expressed in the quoted biblical sentence. Such a negative conclusion has several advantages: It facilitates the understanding of some neurotic symptoms and especially some of the puberty fears of adolescent boys. I remember clearly the case of a patient who had as a boy of twelve a dream in which he had sexual intercourse with a girl. He experienced his first nocturnal emission of semen during the dream. When he woke he felt sad and his depression lasted for days. He was convinced that he had lost his whole virility in that single emission and he was no longer and would never be "a man."

One must strictly differentiate the temporary chastity *ad hoc,* as a sort of universal condition and infallible nostrum for all important and critical junctures,* from the later-developed Christian idea and ideal of chastity. Compare, for instance, those restrictions of savage tribes with the picture St. Jerome gives of his sufferings in writing to the virgin Eustochium (*Enc.* XXII, 87). Here are a few sentences describing his struggles for abstinence:

> Oh, how many times when in the desert, in that vast solitude which, burnt up by the heat of the sun, offers but a horrible dwelling to monks, I imagined myself among the delights of Rome! I was alone, for my soul was full of bitterness. My limbs were covered by a wretched sack, and my skin was as black as an Ethiopian's. Every day I wept and groaned, and, if I was unwillingly overcome by sleep, my lean body lay on the bare earth. I say nothing of my food and drink, for in the desert even invalids have no drink but cold water, and cooked food is regarded as a luxury. Well, I, who out of fear of hell had condemned myself to this prison, companion of scorpions and wild beasts, often seemed in my imagination among bands of girls. My face was pale with fasting and my mind within my frigid body that already seemed to be dead. Then, deprived of all help, I threw myself at the feet of Jesus, washing them with my tears and drying them with my hair, subjugating my rebellious flesh by long fasts. I remember that more than once I passed the night uttering cries and striking my breast until God sent me peace.

No Hebrew man nor any of the males of savage tribes suffered so much (if at all) under the yoke of sexual continence. In this direction the late Christian attitude can well be compared to the behavior of adolescent boys struggling for abstinence. It provides, so to speak, a re-

---

* See A. E. Crawley's article on chastity in *Encyclopedia of Religion and Ethics*, Vol. III, p. 481.

ligious or collective analogy to the individual behavior pattern of many boys at puberty.

64. My second group of observations can best be prefaced by the often-quoted sentence of Oscar Wilde to the effect that "woman is a sphinx without a riddle." Our point of departure is a question: Is not the core of that sentence the unconscious notion that woman is a being without a penis? This conception would hardly sound strange to a writer who was homosexual. His sexual inversion was certainly to a great extent determined by the fact that he missed the male genital in the woman.

But let us turn back to that composite monster, the Sphinx, as we meet it in Egyptian and Greek art. Let me freely confess here that I also have a personal interest in that regression. More than forty-five years ago I delivered a lecture on Oedipus and the Sphinx before the Vienna Psychoanalytical Association.* It was then pointed out that the early type of those enigmatic Egyptian sphinxes were rarely female in their original form. In their rigid gaze they look different from the many female sphinxes from the middle and late Kingdoms of Egypt. The experts say that the female sphinx form acquired its importance in Greece. But even the female sphinxes, possessing the face and breasts of a woman, seem to be strange to the observer. Mephisto admits in the Classic *Walpurgisnacht* of *Faust:*

> *Du bist recht appetitlich oben anzuschauen,*
> *Doch unten hin, die Bestie macht mir Grauen.*

> [Above the waist your looks are most inviting,
> But lower down I find the beast afrighting.]

* On November 2, 1919. Published in No. 2 of *Imago* 1920 and in my book *Dogma and Compulsion,* New York, 1951.

Later forms of the Sphinx can be described as hermaphroditic. In very ancient times of Egypt the male sphinxes
appeared with increasing frequency.

What can be learned from the selective development of
those enigmatic beings? Several things. They were originally male monsters, statues of a lion's body with the
head of a man, ram, or hawk. It seems that this form was
later replaced by or combined with the female form.

Now we turn again to individual development, especially that of the boy. We know that the little boy attributes
to every being a penis like his own. (My son Arthur as a
little boy thought even that a table had a "wee-maker," as
he called his male organ.) Only hesitantly would he accept
the idea that females do not possess that highly valued
male part. The conception awakened in him the dark but
powerful castration-anxiety. He arrived finally at that conclusion on a detour over a compromise—for instance that
the little girl's penis will grow later on. Here is thus an
analogy to the notion of hermaphroditic form. The increasing frequency of the female Sphinx-forms in Greece
thus marks the final acceptance of the notion of the sexual
difference of the female. It cannot be accidental that the
Greeks, who were more inclined to homosexual attitudes
than other ancient peoples, acknowledged this.

After this long detour we return to our point of departure: Did we not venture to guess that the core of that
sentence of Oscar Wilde (woman as a sphinx without a
riddle) is the unconscious astonishment about a human
being without a penis? This at first incredible-sounding
suggestion now gains more plausibility when we compare
the collective development of the Sphinx figure with the
individual concepts of the little boy. Here again is an
analogy from the area of folklore to the individual evolu-
tion. Here is an interesting and perhaps far-reaching addi-

tion and complement to Freud's psychoanalytic theories.

In a corner of my mind is an additional observation contributing to a piece of Freud's theories. Material in dreams often symbolizes women's bodies. The high appreciation women bestow on material things as well as the emotion they show when they see a chair or table damaged seems to confirm such symbolic significance. In this case, even etymology ascertains confirmation: *material* is derived from the Latin word *materia*, which has the same root as *mater*—mother.

The last addition to Freud's theories presents a confirmation from the side of clinical psychoanalysis, a case of neurosis. My patient, a girl in her late twenties, had for three years been having an affair with an older married man who had four children and was unwilling to divorce his wife and marry his mistress. His behavior suggested that a cooling down of their relations would be welcome. When he neither visited nor phoned her for two weeks, she decided to telephone him. It was not he, but his youngest child, a little boy, who answered her. The disappointed girl took an overdose of barbiturates and was brought to the hospital where she slowly recovered: a clear case of a suicidal attempt by poisoning.

Freud pointed out that women prefer poisoning and drowning to other modes of suicide and gave the psychoanalytic explanation that both have an unconscious connection with impregnation. During the psychoanalytic sessions of this particular case it became clear that the girl who had heard the voice of the little boy on the telephone unconsciously wished to have a child like him from the beloved man. Her self-poisoning amounted to an unconscious fulfillment of this wish and simultaneously expressed her utmost despair about the hopelessness of her relations with him.

65. *Memories of Freud:* When as secretary of the Vienna Psychoanalytic Society, I asked Freud before the meeting of the Psychoanalytic Congress at The Hague what I should announce as the subject of his lecture there, he answered that he did not know it yet. Later on he told me that he had thought through all his ideas, sorted them, and considered possible arguments against them on the long evening walks he took through the streets of Vienna. Thus everything was ready in his mind before he ever began to write his paper. The manuscripts he sometimes showed me contained scarcely any corrections, perhaps only a few additions after reading them before sending them to the printer.

Freud often quoted Goethe—especially when, late in his life, he was surrounded by the intimate circle of his students: *"Das Beste, was du wissen kannst, darfst du den Buben doch nicht sagen"* [The best of what you know you are not permitted to impart to the knaves!]. What did he mean? From impressions I got in private conversations with him I would guess he meant: "Enjoy life. Throw away all superfluous and conventional scruples. Enjoy whatever life has to offer to you, especially sexual intercourse!" The dark background against which such remarks stood out, was, of course, the menace of death.

Freud, otherwise very careful in his ways of verbal expression, could occasionally use four-letter words, especially when in conversation with friends or with students he liked. Two such occasions made a lasting impression upon me: one from the time when I was a young student of psychoanalysis and the other from the time I saw Freud to say "Good-by." During a walk we took together in Vienna, Freud reproached me because I was splitting up my energy and work in writing little articles

and book reviews instead of concentrating all on a psychoanalytic paper or on an important subject. "Why," he said,
"do you piss around instead of standing in one place and
pissing there?"

When I saw Freud for the last time he seemed very ill
and to be suffering from the cancer that had been tortur-
ing him for so long. During our conversation he did not
complain, but a pessimistic attitude toward life at the
time comes to a clear expression in the sentences he said
then: "Life is like a baby-shirt: short and full of shit [*kurz
und beschissen*]."

It should, however, be added that those pessimistic moments were rare and easily explainable by his illness. One
thinks of Ernest Renan's words: *"Il se pourrait que la
verité fut triste"* [It could be that the truth might be sad].

In connection with my memories of Freud I recall an
anecdote that amused him very much. It circulated in
Vienna, where it was told about the prominent professor
of dermatology, Moritz Oppenheim (born 1876). This
physician was consulted by an aristocratic lady who was
worried about a skin disease of her eighteen-year-old
daughter. The professor examined the girl, called the
mother in, and said: "I am sorry, your daughter has
syphilis."

"That is not possible!" cried the horrified countess. "She
has never had anything to do with a man. She was educated in Sacre Coeur and the child did not even see a man
there!" But Professor Oppenheim insisted on the correctness of his diagnosis. Finally the countess asked him if it
were not possible that the girl had contacted the infectious
disease on a toilet. Oppenheim replied: "Possible, yes, but
very uncomfortable."

66. *More memories of Freud:* Freud once said in a con-

versation with me that neurotic people look in general much younger than they are and keep their youthful appearance longer than others.

I originally thought that I was constitutionally unable to give a formal lecture and could only present a chat *une causerie* as the French say. Then the memory of my first lecture in the Vienna Psychoanalytic Society came back to me—(1911 or 1912). I read then from a carefully prepared manuscript. On the way home Freud made a few laudatory remarks on the content of the lecture, but scolded me because I had read it from the manuscript. He said that one should make the hearers witness the development of a train of thought and thus seem to improvise a speech. (He was a master of style but not an orator. Those volumes of his writings which someone said "shook the world" were conceived and written after many hours of psychoanalytic practice. He also did not like to give lectures.) Only later on did I become aware of the impression Freud's censuring remarks had made on me. They had, so to speak, put the fear of God into me. I have never since given a formal lecture and have had to restrict myself to chats.

67.   Older man about women: "With women it is as with parking places here in New York. Where do you find in the evening a good parking-place for your car in the city? On this and that corner one is forbidden to park because there is a fire hydrant or a bus stop. There is another good place —and just then another car takes it. Sometimes you see a car move out, but it was a delusion. The driver has changed his mind and stayed there. Finally you decide you will put the car into a garage and let it stay there not only an hour or two, but longer. It costs, of course, a lot more, putting the car into a garage, as it costs much more to marry than to have a passing affair. Finally you must

drive your car from the garage anyhow, and some evenings later you are perhaps searching again for a garage where you can park 'for an hour or two.' "

68. Here is a little experience of my own: I was speaking before a large audience (at the commencement of Sarah Lawrence College, June 1961) and was discussing the three humiliating discoveries that have hurt the pride of men—the findings connected with the names Copernicus, Darwin, and Freud. Suddenly the appropriate expression for those hurts eluded me and I had to use paraphrases. I knew the word quite well: *mortification*. Why had I forgotten it? My train of thought arrived first at the French word *mort* (dead). Only later did the etymology of mortification occur to me: the Latin words *mors* and *facere* —making dead, killing. Here is the analytic explanation: At the beginning of the year before I had a rather serious heart attack and I must have unconsciously feared it could repeat itself. This unconscious fear of dying was thus the main motive of forgetting that word. The repression of the thought of death blocked the way to remembering the term *mortification*. The fact that the first thought occurring to me in my search for the word brought the French *la mort* to the surface, is easily explainable because I had learned French as a boy, many years before I learned to speak English.

Another forgetting of a name is intimately connected with the same fear and unconsciously determined by it. My physician prescribed cortisone pills to combat a skin infection caused by an allergy to a sulfa preparation. Although I knew the name *cortisone* well, I was often much embarrassed when I was in the pharmacy where I always buy my medicine and could not remember the name. As in the previously mentioned case, the forgetting of the name was unconsciously connected with a French word, *cœur. Unconsciously, the name cortisone reminded me* (on account of the similar initial sound) of *coronary*—of the first syllable of my heart attack. The forgetting of the name determined by that memory corresponds to an avoidance of the very unpleasant thought and amounted to the emergence of a fear that the attack could repeat itself. All this although the word *cortisone* has, of course, etymologically nothing to do with *cœur* (heart) and is not a medication for heart disease.

69. Here is another illustrative example of forgetting a name: I became professor of Clinical Psychology at Adelphi University (Garden City, New York) in 1963. Whenever I wanted to mention this fact, I forgot the name Adelphi. Since I like the lecturers and students there, the forgetting cannot be determined by any aversion produced by the new function. In my search for the determining factors the first name that occurred to me was Adelphi (*Adolf* in German), but this is the name of that arch-criminal Hitler who brought to millions of poor people so much misery including some of my own family, not to mention myself. I forgot Adelphi because I connected it mistakenly with the hated name with which it has certainly no relation. The etymological origins and history of the word are, of course, not the decisive factor, but the assonance—Adelphi and Adolf.

70. A writer says: "The other day I had to read a novel I had published five years ago. There was a very vivid discomfort in me during the reading, quite apart from the discontent every writer experiences when he reads one of his books again and recognizes that he should have written it much better. It was not only that, but what I said, there seemed something that not I, but a stranger had expressed and that stranger was really not a very interesting man. At the end I just felt bored and did not give a damn about

what happened to the persons in the novel. Yes, I even wondered how they could interest other readers."

The same author: "I don't doubt that I shall 'arrive,' as they call it. But it is very doubtful when and in what condition. A mountain climber who finally ascends the peak to drop dead there should not be envied."

71. Old man's complaint: "You know, when you are old you often wonder whether your organs are all there, because they are wanting. The legs won't carry me, the intestines don't function well, the penis refuses to get erected."

72. A psychoanalyst relates: "A short time after my patient began to talk in his psychoanalytic session, I took my glasses off and blew at them, cleaning them with my handkerchief. The patient became angry with me because he was convinced that I had yawned. I could not persuade him that I had not done anything of the kind. He insisted that he bores me. It was a clear case of unconscious projection. *He* was bored."

73. Middle-aged man about his children: "I don't understand this whole new generation. They think money is dirty. They also think to make money means to become dirty."

74. Patient: "I had my first erections when I was a boy sliding down the banister in gymnastic exercise."

75. Young man: "I passed by a movie theatre and stood there looking at the woman who was the cashier. She thought I wanted to flirt with her, but I only wondered how she ever got into that paybox, until I assumed that there must be a little door I did not see. Then I wondered if it was not cold for her inside there in the winter."

76. Man about his boss: "He combines the maximum of good intentions with a minimum of common sense."

77. A man, after a discussion with another man:

"Later, at home, I thought about it. It was not that he was wrong in his view that embittered me, but that what he said was partially true."

78. Middle-aged patient to the psychoanalyst: "You always tell me that I must face reality. But I am telling you that the main characteristic of reality is its unpleasantness and I don't want to face that."

79. Psychiatrist: "I sincerely believe that Freud did not properly—that means highly enough—evaluate the power of greed in the human soul."

80. *La petite différence.* From a conversation with an old physician: "You speak of the 'little difference' between men and women. Do you know that Jacques Loeb, one of our greatest medical researchers, said: 'Physiologically men and women are different species'? He meant, of course, as different, let's say, as the tiger and the bear. If this is so, why do you not expect that men and women are also different in their emotional and mental life?"

81. Older man: "I am tired and fed up with that eternal talk about togetherness and often prefer aloneness."

"When I was young, I had an exceptionally good memory. I believe I could have recited the Manhattan telephone book after having read it attentively."

82. "The French say that to depart means to die a little (*c'est mourir un peu*). But to see a dear person leave on the train means more than this: It is as if you were present at his funeral."

83. My first memory of my grandfather is that as a very little boy I was playing in a garden and he asked me what I was doing sitting on the grass. I said: "I am catching that snail" and he replied. "You must hurry up, otherwise it will run away from you."

84. Anthropologist: "The telephone is only the most recent substitute for the tom-toms of African tribes."

85. Middle-aged man: "There are people who hate everybody. At times even themselves, and how right they are!"

"Often the most necessary commodities are most expensive. I now think, of course, of psychoanalytic treatment."

86. Psychologist: "There are no miracles for unbelievers, but there are also no miracles for little children."

87. Bachelor patient: "The grass across the way is not only always greener, but also more alluring to lay down on with a girl. But after it is over, the grass seems to be less alluring than before—and so is the girl."

88. A foreigner who had spent many months in this country observed: "Americans visit so many parties and search for so many opportunities to be with people that they do not even become aware of how lonely they are. They only escape into company."

89. A psychiatrist reporting a consultation with a patient he had seen the day before: "A man phoned me a few days ago from San Francisco and asked me whether I could see him since he would be in New York only for a day. I gave him an appointment and he told me that I had been recommended to him. He came punctually. He was a middle-aged Jewish man. He told me that he had been a very poor boy and had had to work his way up. He had earned money since he was eleven years old. 'I worked furiously,' he said, 'to get money, to secure the best education for my children and to have them and my wife well provided for. I became rich, very rich. I am giving lots of money to Jewish philanthropic institutions yearly. But what's the use? I am now fifty-five years old and I am absolutely impotent for two years. Not only with my wife, but with any woman.'

"I was astonished and asked him why he had not undertaken any treatment at that time and he answered that he could not see a psychiatrist near his town because it would soon be generally known. I advised him to consult a psychiatrist living in a city not too far from his and assured him that this physician, for many years known to me, is reliable, experienced, and absolutely discreet. He asked me then how much he owed me and I answered 'Forty-five dollars.' He took out his wallet and put a hundred-dollar bill on my desk. I wanted to give him his change, but he said 'Leave me alone!' and rushed out."

90. Almost two hundred years ago German writer Jean Paul Richter, now rarely read, wrote: "Sleep, riches, and health, to be truly enjoyed, must be interrupted." This sentence is as psychologically correct as it is astonishing. Self-observation as well as exploration of others confirms its correctness. But why is the interruption necessary? Because only then do we become aware how good it is to sleep, to be rich and to be healthy. Or is it rather the feeling that we do not dream, but that it is reality?

91. *Recurring thoughts.* There are thoughts formed into a short phrase that repeat themselves endlessly. They are as insistent as a phonograph record when the needle has stuck at a certain place.

92. A patient told me a childhood memory in which he saw himself in church listening to a priest who spoke in his sermon addressing the congregation and asking the worshipers what they would do when they met their Maker. The patient, then a little boy, understood the question in the sense of what he would do later when he met his father.

93. Middle-aged patient: "I read a love story yesterday. In it a young man takes a woman out to dinner and a theatre afterward. All is vividly described—their conversations, their intimacy, their impressions, and finally their

lovemaking. Do you know what I missed? There was not a word about the menu in the restaurant and what the two people ate. You laugh? What's funny about it? You remember that Napoleon, who was certainly a great general, once remarked that an army marched on its stomach!"

94. Writer: "No one in America gives a damn about style any longer. The only people who still do are the hair-stylists, I believe."

95. A psychoanalyst, explaining the emergence of unconscious guilt feelings: "Let us assume that you are walking on Broadway and the man before you steps on your toes. You have a corn just there and it hurts agonizingly. You have a single thought toward that stranger: 'Drop dead!' That impulse does not bother you later on. But let us assume that such a violent or murderous thought emerges against your wife, your parents, your children —that's quite different. That impulse percolates within you, has a dynamic effect, causes an emotional conflict. What is the difference in the situation? You don't give a damn about that stranger on Broadway, but you care for your wife, your parents, your children."

96. Lawyer coming from a trial in which he lost his case: "While I drove over here, I thought I had made two mistakes at court. My opponent lawyer was an Irishman, who not only had brazenness but also charm. He began to needle me and I got emotionally involved instead of remaining calm. I could have killed the bastard; that must have been obvious in my answers to him. It did not look good. My second mistake was that in examining the witnesses I was too smart—that means I showed how smart I was. I believe the jurors did not like that."

97. Man in his thirties: "I am living on the remnants of the dreams of glory I had as a teen-ager."

98. Man about a certain woman: "I jealous? Of whom?

One cannot be jealous of a regiment of soldiers or of the population of a suburb."

99. "There are love affairs that are continued after their impetus is entirely exhausted. They are similar to empty peels that had once wonderful fruits in them."

100. Psychoanalyst reporting a case: "I made a serious mistake in fixing my fee. I told the patient the fee would be twenty dollars for each session, but he pleaded with me to reduce it since he did not earn enough. So I charged him only fifteen dollars. Now, almost a year later, when he is very critical of me he sometimes calls me a bargain-basement psychoanalyst."

101. I read in a German book on psychology, written by David Katz and his wife, the interesting and original observations they report about their young son. There are, for instance, good examples of the child's sense of time. The boy, who has heard some biblical stories and who knew that his father had been in the first world war, asked his father David whether he had also fought Goliath. Is it not delightful to hear the boy ask his mother if she also sewed buttons for Father when he was a little boy. The children were told the facts of life, but the boy wanted to know how babies are dressed when they crawl out from mother's body. I heard of a little boy who saw his vaporized breath on a cold winter day coming from his mouth and said to his mother: "Look how dusty I am inside!" What a pity that children's originality of observation and ideas gets lost so soon!

102. Patient recollecting: "In my later teens I thought I had to marry every girl with whom I had sexual intercourse. I now understand in my psychoanalysis that this belief must be traced back to childhood, when I considered sexuality something dirty like urinating and defecating. I must have thought as a child that you do

such dirty things together only after you are married."

103. Man about another: "He is a poet, besides being a teller in the bank. He writes verses, but I doubt that he understands them himself—not to mention others."

About a very old gentleman: "I suppose he became quite senile and tells the same story at each party. I have now heard it several times. If it were only a twice-told tale!"

104. An emotional difference that has been neglected in the psychology of the sexes is the variation of sexual fantasies. Speaking of the average man and woman and putting aside exceptional circumstances (menstrual excitement with women, old age in men), one arrives at the conclusion: In the fantasies of the man, the daydreamer begins with the visualization of sexual situations and only rarely and fleetingly do images of his wooing the woman emerge. Female fantasies in general begin with pictures of the man wooing and admiring her, telling her how much he loves her, giving her sweet names, caressing and kissing her. The transition from affection and love-expressions to sexual excitement is much slower than in the man and progresses gradually. In some female fantasies the restraint of the woman becomes itself a retarding factor. It is then as if her yielding at the end adds to her enjoyment. The attention of psychoanalysts and psychologists has been until now mostly turned to the different behavior patterns of the sexes—their actions before, during, and after sexual intercourse. A psychoanalytic exploration of the differences in the sexual fantasies of the sexes promises to contribute decisive insights into their psychological variations.

105. Old musician: "All you learn comes too late in life. Do you know that Beethoven once said in the period of the last quartets he only then understood how one should

compose? Also for lovemaking one learns the best technique when the faculty for it is vanishing."

106. A psychoanalyst reports in a seminar the case of a homosexual writer whose sexual objects were mostly boys of college age. The man, who had one of his plays successfully performed, was asked by a university to give a course on playwriting. He was now surrounded by young people just of the age and position preferred as love objects by him. The students came to him for advice and guidance in their attempts at writing plays. Although there were many occasions for approaching them, he never touched them and was happy in the role of their teacher and helper. He was himself astonished at his changed attitude and asserted that it was the *eros pedagogicos* (that expression of Plato) that now governed his relation with the young men.

At another time the same man observed: "It is not only intuition that women use when they guess what goes on in a man. It is also shrewd and continued observation. Very little eludes them in the behavior of a man in whom they are interested, and they are using the data revealed in their observations to guide them. They interpret them correctly, often without knowing what those observations were."

107. Middle-aged man: "My physician told me that I am at least ten pounds overweight and that I must restrict my cigarettes to ten daily. I did not want to do this, but then I got that horrible mouth-and-throat infection. I could then swallow only liquid food because other food hurt me. The heat of the cigarette became intolerable in my mouth. Then I felt no desire to smoke. I asked myself whether God is not a malicious demon who fulfills our wishes when it is too late."

108. *A memory of Freud:* Freud insisted that so long as

the guilt feeling of a patient is unconscious one cannot deal with it. It has to become conscious and express its presence and effect in self-damaging actions. It must be above board; otherwise, he said, it is "like wrestling with a Negro in a tunnel." On another occasion he said, with regard to the same dynamic process, "You cannot kill someone who is not present." Only when the guilt feeling is conscious can it be mastered and conquered emotionally.

Here is perhaps the appropriate place to return to that gift of illustrative comparisons so often used by Freud. He once told me that he had learned much about such everyday comparisons from William James, whom Freud had admired when he made James' acquaintance on his trip to the States. We, Freud's Viennese students, often consciously or unconsciously imitated him in such everyday comparisons. I need not say that we were much less successful and original in our attempts. To give an instance of such an attempt, here is a comparison of my own, used to make the dynamics of repression and conscious control clear to students in one of my seminars. I compared the person who represses an unpleasant impulse or idea with a man who stands before the show window of Tiffany's and is tempted to steal a diamond necklace displayed there. The man may tell himself "I could now break into the window and take it" and then consider the consequences of such an action for himself. He will perhaps be caught and end in jail. He could also think of the damage he causes by the theft to others. Perhaps those considerations will prevent him from following his impulse. This case would thus correspond to the process of conscious control. But what would you say if the man, as if he were haunted by Furies, ran down Fifth Avenue away from Tiffany's? This would be analogous to the process of repression, the blind flight away from the forbidden.

109. *Another comparison of Freud:* Freud told us that a family situation in which the mother of a boy is a strict disciplinarian while the father is mild and permissive often creates a preliminary condition for the boy's future homosexual tendencies. He compared that emotional situation and its repercussions to the manner in which the tourist climbs up the Pyramid of Gizeh. This ancient Egyptian pyramid has very high steps. The climbing of the tourist is facilitated by the fact that one Arab stands on the step above the tourist while another stands on the ground. One Arab pulls the tourist up while the other pushes him on. In this manner the visitor of the pyramid progresses. In his comparison Freud pointed out that the strictness of the mother frightens and pushes the little boy away while the mildness and permissiveness of the father attract him.

110. A writer: "Envy of women is rarely felt by men. Here is an exception: I just saw a young woman carrying a baby in her arms across the street. It occurred to me what poor creatures we men are, compared with women. Even when we compose a wonderful symphony, write an excellent play, paint a masterwork or build a grandiose bridge. What is all this compared with creating a baby? We men produce a second best—even in the best instance."

111. Man, late forties, with homosexual tendencies: "I walked on Forty-second Street and looked at men's magazines and fairy pictures, but I checked my impulses because I must preserve my strength for my wife. She does not make many demands on me, it's true. Either she has just started to have her period or she is tired or she has one of her frequent colds."

112. A patient says to the psychiatrist: "It's funny that, to someone who is eccentric or shows bizarre be-

havior, all other people seem odd and incomprehensible.
. . ! What do you mean saying I am out of touch with
reality? Thus are the poets, the great painters, all the most
eminent seekers after truth. If a man should always remain in touch with reality, he would soon become crazy."

113. A patient remembers that she had learned that
when she was six years old her father had been previously
married before he took her mother as his wife. His first
wife had died. The little girl was deeply shocked and felt
very sorry for her mother. She often asked herself: "How
could Father do such a terrible thing to Mother?" The
same patient showed in later life a strange kind of repetition compulsion, the same behavior toward certain situations even when the protagonists were different. Here
are three successive examples of such an attitude: She
had a sexual relationship with a man who was at least
twenty years her senior. This relationship never went beyond the stage of petting. Although she was convinced of
the hopelessness of that relationship for years she could
not break it off. . . . In her badly paid job, in which she
was not promoted, she earned and did the same things in
the first year as in the fourth, and although she realized
clearly that she should leave, she did not. Finally she
went into psychotherapy with a psychiatrist who, as she
understood the situation, did not treat her appropriately.
Nevertheless she could not leave his treatment and stayed
for some years. At the end the three situations were re-
solved by outside agents.

One of the dynamic factors in this woman's strange attitude was, as psychoanalysis showed, her unconscious
identification with the person she should leave (her
almost-platonic lover, her unfriendly boss, her unsatisfactory psychiatrist). She unconsciously took his place
and vicariously imagined how he would suffer if she left

and felt desolate and guilty at the thought. She vicariously took his place: "If I were he——"

114. Psychiatrist in a seminar: "Shakespeare and other poets compare love with psychosis and the lovers with lunatics. I think the comparison with some infectious diseases would be much more appropriate. As you know, some of them have a longer, some a very short incubation. The ways of communicating the diseases are different. Some, such as flu, are transmitted by inhalation. Think of Lohengrin's aria 'Don't you breathe the same airs.' Most of the diseases are spread by contagion. Think of touching the hand of the love object. I shall not enter the discussion of the similarity of symptoms and shall only venture to say that an imaginative physician of the future will find that the typical attack of fever is also a means of defense. Please don't think that that comparison is arbitrary! The same William Shakespeare lets a character in Antony and Cleopatra say:

> Henceforth,
> The white hand of a lady fever thee
> Shake thou to look out.

115. Man and woman are like two planets that move in different orbits and meet on their path only sometimes.

116. Patient, about another young man whom he accuses of being cruel to women: "He got quickly tired of that girl and left her. He said to her: 'You should go out with many young men!' He threw her, so to speak, to the wolves."

"I read that Madame de Staël, who was very ugly, had beautiful arms and she liked to show them bare. She said: 'One shows one's face where one has it.'"

117. *In the beginning:* The best advice one can give to a young psychoanalyst when he starts treating patients is:

Wait and see and hear. He must learn to check his therapeutic zeal and his wish to see the patient improved. That advice was already anticipated by one of Napoleon's ministers, who said: "It's urgent to wait."

118. *Discipline:* A teacher could not maintain discipline in her classroom and the pupils were often defiantly riotous. Although she understood intellectually by what means she could assert her authority, she was unable to do it. When she once, in an analytic session, spoke of the necessity of self-discipline, some childhood memories emerged showing that she had been for a long time a rebellious and unmanageable child. Her difficulty now is particularly related to her unconscious identification with her pupils.

119. *The invisible bridge:* The patient, a young single girl, is very jealous of her boy friend, with whom she has sexual relations. Yet she herself introduced him to various girls with whom he began an affair and thus unconsciously promoted the relations between her boy friend and them.

The case is essentially not much different from that of two soldiers who go together to a brothel and have intercourse with the same prostitute. Both are latent homosexuals; in both cases the same object forms an unconscious, invisible bridge between the two.

120. *Not to speak of oneself:* The great French actor Coquelin used to say that he never spoke of himself (*"Je ne parle jamais de moi"*) and added "Why?" He then gave a long explanation about that characteristic feature of never speaking of himself. Such are the devious ways of self-love.

121. Baudelaire once described the behavior of Victor Hugo in Brussels: The novelist threw himself into one of those long monologues he called a conversation. At many

parties you will run into people who drag you into conversation of this kind, a conversation in which you have not the slightest chance to get a word in edgewise.

122. *A Waltz:* around 1900 a waltz became famous in Paris. The text was

> *En vain dans mes yeux distraits*
> *Tu cherches à lire en moi-même,*
> *Tu voudrais savoir si je t'aime*
> *Mais tu ne saurais jamais.*

perhaps translatable as:

> In my wondering eyes
> You seek to read below
> Wanting to know if I love you,
> But you will never know.

Jean Cocteau, who remembered those lines (in his eulogy on Colette in 1955), thinks their success is determined by the expression of the *grande tactique* of women. They are able to make believe they love a man they don't love, and to disguise it when they do love him.

123. *Dialogue fragment:* Husband in a tiff: "The thing you want to save most in an emergency is your face." Wife: "Wouldn't any woman? That's the most important part she has got."

124. *Another dialogue fragment:* Guest who came a bit early, to the hostess: "How are you?" Hostess: "Generally all right, but today depressed." Guest: "When one is as well dressed as you are this evening, one cannot be very unhappy."

125. Chief of psychiatric clinic, explaining why there are no beds free for female patients and many for male patients: "Yes, it is true that women are more and more

easily subjected to emotional and mental disturbances. When you asserted this, gentlemen, you were correct, but I am afraid you neglected a sociological factor. A woman is easily replaced by another woman, but a man is the breadwinner and everybody hesitates to send him to a psychiatric clinic and keep him there."

126. Philosophical patient: "Marital fidelity is something like religion. Faithfulness of married men need not even be discussed. In this area we arc all alike, undiluted atheists. It is a little different with the fidelity of women. Many people still believe in it, but the majority of our population are unbelievers."

127. "In some instances a loss of face amounts to a gain, at last when you take it literally in the case of very ugly women."

128. Old man: "Not to do anything is perhaps the best way to do something about a critical situation."

"Civilities are sometimes the only tender bridge between people; when those collapse, they become aware that they stand on widely separated shores of a river."

129. Man on a very hot day in the summer of 1963: "When I came over on a bus I observed a young woman who ascended it just before me. She wore slacks, but when she stepped up, she lifted them as if they were a skirt. The power of habit, isn't it?"

130. Young man: "The single girl of today is essentially a security-huntress, and if she does not hunt security, she is worse."

131. Masochistic patient: "It seems I am only happy when I am unhappy." This sentence was quoted by a psychotherapist who reported the case in a seminar and pointed out that the patient could have violent reactions. If he was, for instance, maliciously and openly attacked, he slapped the face of someone, but he then took an ex-

aggerated revenge on himself. In withdrawing the arm, he smashed his elbow against a door in such a way that he had to be hospitalized for several weeks.

132. Young man: "I hate minority groups—Negroes, Jews, Puerto Ricans, and so on. They must be awful people by virtue of the social position they are in."

133. Psychoanalyst reporting a case in a seminar: "The patient was at first compelled to turn every thought he had into action. He was thus, it seemed to me, unable to think before acting. When, for instance, he said: 'I then went out,' he had to get up from the couch as if he wanted to leave. Or when he told me 'I drove through the Holland Tunnel,' he ran his hand through the pillow as if acting out the tunnel drive. Later on he learned that one can think without acting. It has occurred to me that Freud called thoughts actions in small quantities. In this particular case, thoughts were still closer to actions and reactions than in others."

134. It cannot be accidental that women in general are more cautious than men on the street and that they have fewer accidents at home and outside. Their function is to preserve life, their own and that of the next generation. It would certainly be worth while to explore the psychological differences of the two sexes in that direction.

135. Man: "I sat and observed the people during the party. There is a saying 'If glances could kill—' I have not seen such glances except a few among some women who were competing with each other. But I observed the glances exchanged between women and men and I had a funny idea: 'If glances could mean sexual intercourse, life would be an uninterrupted and promiscuous orgy.'"

136. Pathetic comment of the wife of an alcoholic: "I wish he would look at me with such desire as he does at

that bottle of whiskey. I wish he would feel the same pricklings of his fingers when he touches my body as when he reaches for the bottle. It is nice for a woman to feel wanted."

137. *Self-evaluation.* We are accustomed to the notion, prevalent in our culture pattern, that a woman's self-evaluation is also determined by the nature of the male "company she keeps." For easily understandable reasons, men in general apply a different standard to their self-evaluation. Yet in exceptional cases men also think less of themselves when they have women of inferior qualities. A thirty-one-year-old patient who has considerable difficulties with his sexual potency was in such a situation. His mistress was vulgar, unmanageable, indiscriminately promiscuous—and did not conceal it. The man complained during a psychoanalytic session: "I must be pretty lowdown when I have no one to go out with but that piece of garbage."

138. This patient's behavior puzzled and mystified me for a longer time because he did not dare approach women sexually, and was also inhibited and shy with them socially. Identification with women and masochistic trends appeared in his fantasies. He also procrastinated in his profession and had great difficulty in completing the tasks he tackled. The first insight into the puzzle of his behavior came, surprisingly enough, in the interpretation of one of his dreams: "I was again on First Avenue where I lived as a boy. I had two suitcases with me, but some boys took them away from me and tossed them to each other. I tried to get them back but could not." His thought associations to this dream were not significant, memories from his early boyhood and of fighting with other boys. A day-remnant he remembered was that he had recently carried two valises, and so on. "Listening with the third

ear" to the patient, I was myself surprised by a strange thought that had occurred to me; namely that the two valises symbolically represent the testicles. Without entering into the discussion of the other dream content, I told the patient that my impression was that as a child he had had undescended testicles. To my great astonishment he said that he had just thought of the same thing, a physical handicap of his early years which was not overcome before he became thirteen. He said he had once told me about this at the beginning of his psychoanalytic treatment, but I had no memory of it. It is very likely that he had wanted to tell me but didn't. This is the more probable because he admitted that he had always avoided the subject, even in his thoughts, whenever possible. His hesitations and indecision as well as his fantasies became clearer in their unconscious motivations by this surprising light thrown on his prepuberty years with their shameful feelings.

The genesis of my startling interpretation of the patient's dream can be perhaps helped by a reconstruction I attempted later on. Many years before this patient had come to me, I had once treated a man who as a boy was burdened with the same physical handicap. During an analytic session that patient had once quoted the Latin sentence *Omnia mea mecum porto* [Everything that is mine I carry with me], alluding to his now-normal sexual organ. The preconscious memory of that case and the thought-connection between personal possessions carried and the two suitcases must have paved the way to the dream interpretation.

139. *Vision of the future:* I foresee a future in which churches, temples, mosques, and other houses of worship have disappeared and have made room for hospitals, homes for the poor and the aged, for children deserted by

their parents, and other underprivileged people. The amount saved from not building houses of worship will then be spent on those buildings, dedicated to the true religion of mankind.

140. *Dream interpretation:* The patient begins his psychoanalytic session with the report of this dream: "I dreamed that you and I were exchanging shoes. Mine were very dirty and yours clean. After the change your shoes were full of mud, but mine were clean." The patient has no helpful thought associations to the dream and speaks of other things, particularly of his present lack of money. The meaning of the dream remains puzzling so long as one does not remember that mud, stool, and so on in dreams are symbols of money. Connecting the last association [lack of money] of the patient, the analyst could give the following dream interpretation: The patient says, using the dream symbolism: At first I had money enough and you were poor, now we have changed places. The patient admits that he sometimes thought that he wanted to be "in the analyst's shoes."

141. *A child's thought:* A three-year-old girl was often warned she should be cautious and not swallow a cherry stone. The child once swallowed one and knelt down before a crucifix, praying that God should make it leave her body through the opening of the bowels and not let a cherry tree grow within her.

142. Viennese patient: "The Viennese have a saying —'Love travels through the stomach'—that amounts to a fair warning to the wife to cook well because if she does her husband will love her. I have had pressure in my stomach since yesterday. Now I do not know if my wife does not love me any more or whether she is merely a bad cook. I only know that I don't love her at the moment."

143. Wary bachelor: "The danger of playing with fire

is, of course, of getting burned. That is valid also for play-ing with the fire of sexual desires. But how about that formidable group of women—you know them as teasers —who play with the fire of men. These women not only light the fire, they also add fuel to it and find great satis-faction in observing it. They let others burn. Whenever I tune in on one of them, I am tempted to cry 'Fire!' "

"I now expect the publication of one of those do-it-your-self books with the title *How to Succeed With Women Without Really Trying.*"

144. *Viennese mentality after Hitler:* A few years ago I returned to my birthplace for a few summer weeks. The city is still beautiful, the environs even more so. The food is as good as before and the view from Kahlenberg in the evening over the Danube will enchant anyone. But the people, friendly as always, are provincial. There are many religious processions and men in native Austrian costume (naked knees and *lederhosen*). The Nazis left their imprint—even in the language of the advertisements (*Zweitschrift* instead of *Kopie*).

I met an old acquaintance on the street. This man, I am sure, was one of the first who greeted Hitler's entrance in Vienna and became at least *Obersturmführer* under the Nazis later on. "You had it easy," he told me, "living in free America, while we here had to suffer under Hitler!" The Viennese were always hypocrites in this way; they were, as the Viennese often called it themselves, *Schnitt-lauch auf jeder Suppe* [leaves of chive, used as season-ing in every soup].

An American visitor came to Vienna in the autumn of 1962. This lady wanted to buy some oranges and could not find any. (She spoke excellent German.) Finally she asked a fruiterer about the absence of oranges. The man answered: "The Italian oranges did not yet arrive and I don't take those from Palestine because they stink of Jews."

145. *Cinderella:* Freud told us that the dream and other products in which the unconscious has the decisive part bring to light material which we have to regard as part of the archaic heritage, which a child brings with him to the world—before any experience of his own—as an experience of his ancestors. Freud considered, for instance, dream symbols as such inherited experience; he told us that the dreamer does not know their meanings and the psychoanalyst who interprets a dream has to acquaint the patient with the significance of those symbols.

I do not doubt the archaic origin of the symbols, or their significance, but I doubt recurrently and seriously whether their latent meaning is entirely unknown to us or (better put) whether we do not unconsciously understand their significance.

I shall advance the argument by presenting two instances in which there appears the same symbol, whose meaning we seem to understand or to conceive at least unconsciously or preconsciously. The first example comes from the rich treasure of old folk stories. Everybody knows the fairy tale of Cinderella, the beautiful drudge who had to serve her rich relatives. The tale tells us that the girl, favored by a fairy godmother, was sent, wonderfully dressed, to the ball where a prince fell in love with her. Cinderella wore glass slippers when she went to the ball. In her hurry to return home at midnight, she dropped one of the slippers. The prince took it and searched for the girl whose foot fit the slipper precisely. He found Cinderella and married her.

No reader of or listener to this fairy tale will deny that the story of the slipper and the foot has a symbolic sexual significance the meaning of which can easily be explained:

The slipper represents the vagina, the foot the penis. The prince married the girl into whose genitals his penis fits well. Is there not a preconscious understanding of that symbolism in each of us?

The second instance is taken from clinical psychoanalysis. A patient who had intensive but cleverly disguised tendencies toward shoe fetishism reported that on the long bus ride to my office he had sat across from a young woman. The whole time he stared at the girl's shoes as if he were fascinated by them. He never looked at her face or figure—only at her shoes. Not his behavior but that of the young woman interests us here. She became visibly and acutely embarrassed by his concentration on her shoes. As he described it, she tried at first to conceal her confusion but then betrayed her embarrassment and blushed. The patient stated that had she, like women in earlier times, worn a long dress she would certainly have withdrawn her shoe under it in order to avoid his looking at it. She would, he said, have hidden it as if she were ashamed of it. She would have shut the shoe off from sight as if it were a naked sexual object.

It can scarcely be doubted that the behavior of the young woman on the bus shows that she preconsciously or unconsciously understood the symbolic meaning of the shoe and reacted to it as a girl would to the sexual observation of a voyeur.

146. *Transformations of masochism:* A very intelligent young woman, a high school teacher, could not reach a climax in sexual intercourse except when she had masochistic fantasies—for example that she, being Jewish, was a prostitute who had to be at the disposal of Nazi soldiers. In psychoanalytic treatment those fantasies receded and finally disappeared, but in their place emerged a conspicuous change of behavior. The girl became promiscuous

and on a first date went to bed with any man who wanted her. This behavior had, of course, the result that men treated her with contempt and soon deserted her. She had given up her masochistic fantasies but now became masochistic in her life.

At the root of her masochism was her self-punishment for unconscious murderous impulses against her mother, with whom she lived in a continuous, terrible conflict. She herself often conceived the relationship as a tug of war in which she and her mother were joined together by the navel-string on which they pulled.

147. *Memories of pre-Hitler Vienna:* One day, contrary to habit, I looked at the pictures in the vestibule of my apartment before I left it. There are some photographs of the men who were important to me when I was a student—pictures of Dostoievsky and Schopenhauer, of Gustav Mahler and Anatole France, of Beer-Hofmann and Arthur Schnitzler. There is also a small reproduction of Giorgone's *Concerto* with its three figures, one of which shows a striking resemblance to young Gustav Mahler. (The picture was also in Mahler's office when he was director of the Vienna Opera.) On the bookcase stands, dominating all else, the bust of old Goethe. My glance lingers a bit on the photograph of Schnitzler and on the lines he had written below it:

Tiefsinn hat nie ein Ding erhellt
Klarsinn blickt tiefer in die Welt.

Perhaps translatable as:

By profound thought no thing was ever clarified,
Clear thought pervades the world with deeper light.

For a moment I look again into his steel-blue eyes and listen to his voice as I did so often on our walks in

Vienna. Recently I read the commemorative speech on Schnitzler by Franz Werfel (*Neue Rundschau* 1931), who calls the poet "master of loneliness" and contends that "loneliness forms the essential content of all his works and characters, from the first to the last. . . ." A remark Schnitzler once made to me came to mind: "One can feel really lonely only in company."

My son Arthur is named after Schnitzler, who took some interest in the boy. We lived in Vienna in the Sternwartestrasse—as did Arthur and Olga Schnitzler, who sometimes invited me to dinner at their hospitable home. Afterwards we walked in the garden. One of my books, *Arthur Schnitzler als Psychologe* (1912; not translated into English), explores his novels and plays with the methods of psychoanalysis.

Beside Schnitzler's photograph is one of Beer-Hofmann with a dedication to me dated May 1919. I was only twenty-two when I wrote a little book about that great poet, who has remained almost unknown in America. He was one of Schnitzler's best friends. I was often a guest in his house, over the portal of which was chiseled the star of David. A line from his "The Young David" comes back: "Also for a people it is not worth while to live only for themselves." Rainer Maria Rilke once remarked that Beer-Hofmann presented "the grandeur and dignity of Jewish destiny." (Apropos Rilke another memory emerges. I was then an Austrian army officer and was present when the poet was called to military service in the first world war. A typically Viennese sergeant took down the personal data. "What's your name?" asked the sergeant. "Rainer Maria Rilke." The sergeant, who did not understand this, rebuked Rilke. "What do you mean *Maria?* I don't call myself Mizzi.")

Leaving the house, the memory of the photograph of Mahler on the wall of my antechamber followed me. And suddenly a little experience, long forgotten, surfaced in memory. It must have been in the winter of 1907, shortly after I had heard Mahler's Second Symphony for the first time. A few evenings later I came from the Opera and walked down the Ringstrasse. I knew that Mahler walked behind me and I whistled. I was a nineteen-year-old student at the Vienna University at the time. Suddenly Mahler was beside me and asked: "What did you whistle just now?" I answered: "The waltz theme from your Second Symphony." "Good," said Mahler, pleased; shook my hand; and tramped along with his peculiar gait.

Perhaps twenty years later, I was a guest at Mahler's house in Breitenstein, where Werfel and Alma Mahler then lived. I had been introduced to them by Baron Dirsztay and we spent a wonderful day and evening on the Semmering taking long walks in the woods.

Those memories were, of course, not all revived while I now took a walk. I decided to visit my younger daughter Miriam (named after Beer-Hofmann's "Lullaby for Miriam") who was studying for her Ph.D. at Columbia and lived not many blocks from us. While Miriam and I drank coffee together, I looked at the walls of her apartment and saw there beautiful original letters of Freud, Einstein, and Thomas Mann. Here hung the "lullaby for Miriam," translated into English, with a few cordial words to me from Beer-Hofmann, who was then (1942) already in New York, where I saw him. And there was Beer-Hofmann's beautiful poem "The Lonely Road" with the poet's lines underneath: *For Theodor Reik in memory of past days, most cordially.*

On the other wall was the recommendation Freud

wrote in October 1933 when I moved from Vienna to The
Hague. That one is already published,* but shouldn't the
letters of Mann and Einstein be copied and be made
known? Especially the critical letter of Mann might interest many people. I must have asked Mann for a few
lines of a preface for my book on Goethe, which he knew
and which I wanted to publish in English.† His answer is
dated Princeton, 21.I. 1941:

> Dear Dr. Reik:
> What you suggest honors me, but I cannot do what you
> want me to. I feel actually overburdened and must make
> a great effort to do my personal work beside the daily de-
> mands of this time. "The trials increase with the years,"
> Goethe remarks, and it is badly arranged that, so long as
> one is young, one is on the zenith only relating to sports
> and has really nothing to accomplish and later on so much.
> "A few lines"—that is easily said, but when I once begin
> to write, I get involved and it becomes work which I can-
> not now afford. In Goethe's world I was enclosed for a
> long time. Although I shall never desert this very world,
> I do not want to return to the problem-sphere of written
> books—I mean, the Lotte–Goethe novel.*
> I had already read your Friederike study before and
> have now again looked at it with admiration for your
> thematic abundance and for your daring in it performed
> according to the analytic principle *aude sapere*. Should
> I add that the insights into those depths which are not
> deeper than sex (but this is a well very deep) sometimes
> affects one as a little monotonous and the valor which
> Freud attributes to you has something customary and
> specialistic? This remark comes into my pen although I

---

* In my book *The Search Within,* New York, 1952, p. 653.
† Published as *Fragment of a Great Confession,* New York, 1949.
‡ I had asked if I should include a paper on Goethe's *Faust* in the
book. I did not.

feel what psychoanalysis has given me, and because I fight
shy of the specialization in it without detracting from all
feelings of obligation and alliance which I have toward it.

In conclusion: I would not however attractive it is include the Faust paper in the book because of formal reasons and because it would also damage the subject.

With best regards and wishes

Yours sincerely
Thomas Mann

The polemical and critical remarks in this letter are certainly of greater interest than those laudatory of my book.

To conclude those memories, here is a letter dated Jan-
uary 6, 1941, from Albert Einstein, to whom I had sent
my books *From Thirty Years with Freud* and *Masochism
in Modern Man:*

> Dear Mr. Reik:
>
> I thank you very much for sending me your books. I
> have already finished reading with great interest the book
> on masochism; it appears to me very convincing. What I
> have read so far in the book on Freud I liked very much.
> It offers much more than a biography in the usual sense
> and will certainly contribute to promote the understanding
> of Freud's wonderful personality.
>
> With best regards and wishes
>
>
>
> Your
> *A. Einstein*
>
>

148. *A diagnosis of Freud:* Here is a story predating
Freud's writing of his book on lay analysis. In 1924 or 1925,
I had an American patient who was returning, after a
summer vacation, from New York to Vienna to resume her
psychoanalytic treatment. On board ship this woman
made the acquaintance of a man, also from New York,
whom she understood was suffering from some emotional
disturbances. She advised him to consult Freud. Freud

saw him in consultation and referred him to me. He had
given the patient a visiting card for me on which was written: "Z.W. Full psychoanalytic treatment." (Z.W. was an
abbreviation for the German *Zwangsneurose*—obsessional neurosis.)

I began the psychoanalytic treatment and it seemed
that the patient really did have a developed obsessional
neurosis. There were many doubts and undoubtedly obsessional thoughts concerning many subjects. The obsessional neurosis was, so to speak, on the surface. After three
months ˙ psychoanalytic treatment the symptomatology
of ˙¹ patient changed surprisingly. He had in the mean-
t˙ ᴊe begun an affair with a woman and complained that
his sexual potency was disturbed. Later on he expressed
the suspicion that I wanted to castrate him. He then had
delusions and asserted that certain men came over the
roof and wanted to break into his room. He got into a violent quarrel with the landlord and finally went to the
American consul to accuse me. It was clear that his obsessional neurosis covered paranoia.

The prosecutor made a preliminary inquiry that did
not lead to any results. In the Viennese newspaper only
short notices about the case were published. Freud wrote
a letter to the *Neue Freie Presse* (comparable to *The New
York Times*) in which he presented a short statement.
He declared that he had referred the case to me because
he had special confidence in me in the treatment of difficult cases of this kind. (Freud's daughter Anna was also
mentioned in this letter since he referred cases of another
kind to her.)

The patient came to me, to the best of my recollection,
in September 1924. *Die Frage der Laienanalyse* was published in September 1926 (American translation, *The
Problem of Lay-Analysis,* New York, 1927).

149. *Freud and Beer-Hofmann:* Freud and the great Austrian poet Richard Beer-Hofmann both lived most of their lives in Vienna without meeting. They had common friends, especially Lou Salome, who became a student of Freud whom he liked and whose talents he highly appreciated. Lou Salome was an intimate friend of Beer-Hofmann's family. When Hitler came to Vienna, Beer-Hofmann finally visited Freud. Beer-Hofmann told me about this visit much later when he was in New York. Both men discussed the Jewish question and, of course, the situation in Vienna. Freud knew all that Beer-Hofmann had written.

I had already published a little book on Beer-Hofmann in 1911 (the first book of a twenty-three-year-old man) in which Freud's name occurred in connection with dream interpretation. When a second, changed edition of this little book appeared, Freud reproached me because I had not sent it to him.

Case of a sexual masochist: In my book *Masochism in Modern Man** I described the case of a sexual masochist who later found the transition to a form of social masochism. The man had been a patient of Freud for three years and had in this time conquered his perverted sexual tendencies. When Freud referred him to me for continuation of the treatment, I was a young and inexperienced psychoanalyst. The patient who had been analyzed by Freud for so long could have taught me certain things and his report of the sessions with Freud gave me some valuable psychoanalytic insights. Nevertheless I could help him considerably later on to overcome his emotional disturbances. He showed his gratitude in dedicating to me a novel he had written after the end of his psychoanalytic treatment.

* First published in 1941 by Farrar, Straus and Company, New York.

Titled *Der Doppelgänger* [The Second Self], the novel was illustrated by Oscar Kokoschka. The patient, who was Jewish, and his wife committed suicide when Hitler came to Vienna.

This patient was at first sexually impotent, but functioned normally in sexual intercourse later on. During our psychoanalytic sessions we returned, of course, frequently to the problem of the origin and the dynamics of his sexual masochism. During this time something strange happened. He sometimes took a walk on the Kärtnerstrasse in Vienna, a street frequented by high-type prostitutes in the late evenings. The patient in passing sometimes gave those women a little slap on the behind. It once happened that one of the dames turned around and slapped his face. Whereupon the patient very angrily shouted: "Why do you hit me you tramp? I am myself a sadist!"

There was, of course, a large crowd of people; the patient was taken to the police and had to appear at court. Freud and I were called to court as experts; if memory does not fail, the patient got away with a fine.

150. *Objectivity of artistic discrimination:* I do not believe in objectivity of opinions about art works. Not to mention other reasons, could you have an objective opinion, let me say, about the poem or the sculpture of your worst enemy? Could you form a cool and dispassionate opinion about paintings made by a man who has seriously hurt your feelings? Subject to all human frailties, would we not in our opinion be influenced by antipathy and hostility?

Not each of us would in such a case be as sincere (naïve?) as the great composer Anton Bruckner, concerning whom I recently heard a telling anecdote. He had listened attentively to a Mass at the church at Steyer. When the Mass was finished, he said to the choirmaster:

"That's beautiful music. Who wrote the Mass?" The choir-master named the Viennese musical theoretician Dr. Joseph Marx as the composer. "What?" cried Bruckner, "Marx composed it? He still owes me a florin, the cad! No, his music does not amount to much. I would have to lie if I said that I liked the Mass!"

Fully to appreciate that anecdote, one has to imagine the rapid transition from gladness to gloom and the sentences said in Anton Bruckner's broad Austrian dialect.

151. *Emotional disturbance of a child:* A woman psychologist reported the case of a nine-year-old girl who refused to go to school except when her mother went with her and stayed in the class or nearby. The girl often shouted: "Mummy, Mummy!" When the child's absences became more frequent, the school psychologist decided that the child should leave this school and go to another for disturbed children. The mother could not, of course, always stay in school with the daughter. When the child had again stayed away from school for a few days, the school psychologist, who was in conflict with the child's psychotherapist, fixed a deadline for the reappearance of the girl.

In this emergency situation the therapist made up her mind to tell the girl what she had understood of the case for a long time. The child must have unconscious death-wishes against her mother and her fears of separation from Mother amounted to intensive emotional reactions to those repressed wishes.

The effect of the analytic explanations was that the child felt depressed and turned against the psycho-therapist. Working through the unconscious material, however, resulted in the girl overcoming her resistance; she appeared in the class on the day of the deadline. Since then the child goes to school regularly—without her mother staying with her. This beautiful therapeutic success was gained primarily through the moral courage of the woman psychologist who recognized that the unconscious guilt feeling had to be brought to the surface. The therapist, so to speak, lifted the stone and let her little patient see what was beneath it.

152. *Clothes and sex:* Someone quotes a very early childhood memory from a contemporary novel (*Sol Myers* by Judah Stampfer, New York 1962, p. 1). A man remembers, "My dad wore an apron in front and pants in the back, so I was sure, crawling around, that he was half-man, half-woman."

153. *Jewish Proverb:* There is an old Jewish proverb I heard when I was a little boy: "You ask a sick person, you give a healthy person" [*Einen Kranken fragt man, einen Gesunden gibt man*]. It was said whenever a guest was at our table you should ask a sick person if he is allowed to eat a certain dish, but you shouldn't ask a healthy man. You just serve him.

154. *Childhood memories of Old Vienna:* A man: "When I was sick and slowly recovering, my mother, I remember, sometimes quoted some lines, the mother of Emperor Franz Joseph, Sophie of Bavaria, wrote once on the Esplanade in Ischl, Salzkammergut. She found an inscription there saying that to be healthy is the best thing on earth, but she wrote below:

> *Man sagt, das höchste Glück auf Erden*
> *Ist gesund zu sein.*
> *Ich sage nein,*
> *Das höchste Glück auf Erden*
> *Ist gesund zu werden.*

> [They say the greatest happiness on earth
> Is to be healthy.

I am saying: No!
The greatest happiness here below
Is to recover health again.]

When I was a boy in Vienna, women began to smoke.
My mother hated the sight of smoking women and used
to say: "Every dunghill smokes."

I have nothing against ladies' smoking, but I still don't
like to see them walking in the street doing it. In my
thoughts, such a woman comes close to being a street-
walker.

The most elegant restaurant in Vienna was, of course,
the Hotel Sacher near the Opera. The members of Franz
Joseph's family often were guests there. Mrs. Sacher was
an original person. She knew, of course, all the guests.
Once a lady of light virtue whom she did not know came
in to have dinner. Mrs. Sacher got upset and shouted: "The
Princess Luise of Koburg is the only whore I tolerate in
these rooms."

155. *Assassination of President Kennedy:* We all are
still under the deep impression of the murder of the President. To the many unsolved puzzles a new one was
added. We are told that alleged murderer Lee H. Oswald was as a boy already suspected of being insane.
Whoever followed the report about his behavior will recognize that he was either a paranoiac or a borderline-case.
The questions that confront us, then, are: How was it
possible that such an insane person walked around free?
When a man is suspected of having cholera or typhus,
don't we put him into a hospital and isolate him? We do
this even when the diagnosis is not yet certain, that
means, when only the suspicion of the dangerous disease
exists. And in cases such as Lee H. Oswald's we let dangerous men move freely and unobserved among people?

156.   Man, highly visual type: "Before we write the date 2000, psychoanalysis will have changed its character very radically. By then a person will have his memories on a television apparatus and will be able to show his psychoanalyst how he was as a child or a young man, to show him in a movie what his parents and friends and sweethearts were like. He will also be able to show him a few significant events of his life in pictures."

"I had a cold yesterday and stayed in bed, looking at television. You know, I counted how much a man would spend who would buy everything, from houses and cars to razors, that are announced in commercials. If he buys only one of each recommended article, he would need a million dollars."

157.   A psychologist in a seminar: "I believe that women love better than we men. That is because they see in the man not only himself but also the child they could have from him, his potentialities. They see not only the child in the man, but also their child from this man. This begins in sexual intercourse—or rather long before that. After the orgasm I feel as distant from a woman as if she were on another planet and the woman feels closer to me, more affectionate than before. When she is sick, for instance during her menstruation, the fact that she does not look well reduces my affection for her. But when I happen to be sick, she is not remote. On the contrary, it awakens some maternal feelings for me in her and she is sorry that I look badly."

158.   *Recovery:* When, a few weeks after a serious heart attack, I stood at the window, I made the decision that I would after my recovery enjoy life more than before, spend more money on myself, allow myself to eat some delicacies, travel to Europe again. Yes, even the

thought of women and sexual intercourse emerged. And now, a few months later, none of those promises given to myself have been kept. I eat the same food as before, I don't travel much, and I see women only passing by in the street. Danger and threat to life form exceptional situations; now everyday life has the upper hand again.

159. Psychologist: "It is often much more interesting to follow the irrational mind of a woman than the rational but often not reasonable thoughts of a man."

160. *A dream interpreting itself.* A patient during the psychoanalytic session says: "You said yesterday that I must once as a little boy have observed sexual intercourse by my parents. It's true that I slept in the same room, but I cannot remember such an observation. I don't know why at this moment the dream I had last night occurred to me. It was in that bedroom and my father and mother were there, but not in bed. My father had a big candle and he extinguished it in water. I saw how the wax from the candle dropped into the water."

Not only the succession of this dream after the preceding discussion of a possible observation but also the sexual symbolism of the candle confirm the suggestion of the psychoanalyst.

161. An example of obsessional thinking: "You must have read in the newspapers that at present we in New York have a scarcity of water. The Mayor admonished the people to economize and save water wherever possible. Now I give you an example of my thoughts. Today in the morning I went to the bathroom to urinate. I couldn't at first, no urine came—you know that I have that little prostate trouble. Thus I stood there and waited. It sometimes helps when I open the water-tap a little and let water run. It suddenly occurred to me that I am wasting

water against the orders of the Mayor and, although I had now begun to urinate, I had to interrupt and turn off the water-tap."

162. Man: "I don't believe that even Zeus making love to a mortal woman was dignified."

The same man: "Homosexuality makes even stranger bedfellows than heterosexuality."

163. From a seminar in which the psychology and psychopathology of advertisement were discussed: "The main principle of efficient advertising is that it should fulfill one's wishes. Of course, it should have in the first line the wish to get excellent goods that are not expensive, but besides this conscious wish, unconscious wishes should also find satisfaction in the words and pictures of the advertisement. From this principle one must conclude that expressions that touch on unpleasant and disagreeable thoughts must be avoided."

I remember having seen a picture, considered an advertisement of a firm, in which Jesus is presented hanging on the cross. A Roman legionary proffers him on a spear a sponge with vinegar. From Christ's lips issues a paper on which is written "That's good. That's Brown's vinegar." . . . Do you think that this advertisement will help the sale of Brown's product? Certainly not; not only on account of the blasphemy contained in the picture, but also because it awakens painful thought associations such as death and execution.

Among the unconscious gratifications, an efficient advertisement offers economy in expression, which is important.

Here is an excellent example of such a display: In Berlin before Hitler was a well-known store called Loeser. It had many branches in all parts of the city. Loeser specialized in ladies' shoes and hose. When evening came, all Loeser stores switched on an electrified capital *L* in the shape of a female leg with shoe. It became engraved in women's memories—not only on account of the mnemonic device in which the name *Loeser* is connected with the memory trace of shoe and stockings but also by virtue of the economy of expression, which is unconsciously appreciated.

164. From a seminar in which the unconscious sources of wit and humor were discussed. The speaker, a refugee from Austria, said: "The Austrian army was always carrying on war and there is scarcely any nation in Europe that cannot boast that it has defeated the Austrian army. Even the Swiss defeated the Austrians in 1386. . . . When the first world war started, a Jewish member of Parliament—if I remember correctly, Robert Stricker—sighed: 'I wish we had already lost this war.' "

165. The tragedy of the middle-aged woman, the *femme entre deux âges,* is well expressed in the aria of the Marschellin in Strauss' *Der Rosenkavalier.* Any woman in that age group will occasionally feel as she does: "Sometimes I arise in the dead of night and stop the clocks, each one of them."

166. Remarks on language: A refugee from Germany who learned English after he arrived here reports: "The bus on which I rode was pretty full. There were only two seats besides me free and one seat near the driver. Then a young woman with three children, aged three to ten, came into the bus. I got up from my seat and went to the single seat in order to make room for the young mother and her children. At the next stop she came up to me and said: 'Aren't you nice?' I did not understand the question form and seriously answered: 'I try to be.' My

American friend told me later that the question meant only that the woman wanted to say 'You were nice to get up.'"

167. Only the German language knows the expression *Handschuh* (shoe for the hand-glove). In German the word *Schuld* means debt as well as guilt, a double meaning not existent in English or French.

168. When my son Arthur was a small boy, he had a toy drum which he was beating without stopping. When I told him to stop, he beat it at least once more, so that it appeared that he discontinued because he himself wanted to cease, not because I had ordered him to. Early signs of revolution.

169. Among the manifestations of unconscious guilt feelings, provocation is too little discussed in psychoanalytic literature. The special interest provocation awakens is a result of the double function it serves: It is in most cases an attack (for example against the psychoanalyst during the phase of negative transference) and as such is an expression of violent aggressive and unconscious impulses. On the other hand, it should cause punishment for the provoking person, verbally—and in the unconscious continuation also physically. Here is a pertinent example of the behavior of a five-year-old girl, remembered during her psychoanalytic treatment. She was hiding herself behind the couch while her mother and grandmother were away. When they came home, they anxiously searched for the child, who was lying there without making a sound. The child enjoyed the increasing anxiety of her mother and grandmother, who finally became almost frantic. Grandfather came home, pushed the couch away, and gave the girl a good spanking. The expressions the woman used in telling her childhood reminiscence showed not only the mentioned function of provocation

—she said, for instance, that she "enjoyed" the whole event—but also revealed another one. She said of her grandfather: "He at least cared," betraying that unconsciously she identified being punished with being loved. In her psychoanalytic treatment she often repeated the same pattern of provocation so that it became necessary for the psychoanalyst to tell her that her unconscious aim was to be thrown out of his office.

To the characteristic features of some masochistic personalities belongs a feeling of their own worthlessness that often leads to self-sabotage. A woman teacher who in spite of all indications to the opposite was convinced that she was not good in the classroom unconsciously did many self-sabotaging things in order to lose her job. Her feeling of worthlessness was based on unconscious guilt feeling originating in death-wishes directed against her father and only later transferred to her profession.

170. *On bisexuality:* Uniforms are essentially contrary to the character of femininity because women strive to be dressed differently from one another. Stewardesses, usherettes, and female military personnel must sometimes feel nostalgic for the dresses they could wear, while they perhaps appear to themselves impersonal and anonymous so long as they are uniformed.

171. *Impressions after a symphony concert:* The conductor of the symphony orchestra whom I observed attentively appeared to me suddenly a personified representation of bisexuality. He is, of course, the leader and subject only to the composer whose work he performs; as such he is very masculine. On the other hand, he is in the center of attention and wants to be in the limelight like a woman. While he conducts his right arm beats time and thus commands the orchestra, but his left arm illustrates the character of the music and shows in its

abundance of gestures a definite resemblance to the movements with which women accompany their talking. He leads the orchestra, but in signaling the individual instrumentalists he resembles the lady of the house who, for instance at a party, brings various people into the foreground. He directs, so to speak, the conversation during the party. He calls the tunes as a leader, but he dances with them or seems to dance with them while he conducts, as if he were unable to resist the temptation.

172. *The other side of the coin:* There must be in every woman, even the purest, an occasional fantasy in which she figures as a prostitute, as there sometimes emerges in every man, even in those of the most rigorous morality, the impulse to murder someone.

173. Patient, about a friend: "His friends call him a son of a bitch; what his enemies must call him is unimaginable."

174. Young man: "I am lonely, but so is everybody. I am perhaps only more aware of it than the others."

175. A self-critical patient: "I cannot tolerate hearing my own voice any longer. What I say does not sound as if it would be true sentiment, but sentimentality."

About a friend: "Then I said to him: 'See you later,' but I thought 'In the beyond, but not before it.' "

176. A patient, speaking of religion: "I am quite willing to cast my bread upon the water if it comes back to me changed into a roast-beef sandwich."

"You never know what other people think. More than this—you never know what you, yourself, think."

177. Obsessional patient: "I assure you that the problem of whether I should step into the Senator cafeteria on Ninety-sixth Street or walk down to Steinberg's Dairy instead sometimes becomes for me a question of life and death."

178. When one is not only unwilling but also unable to sin, to speak in theological terms, life becomes less and less valuable. That means when all our appetites dwindle, when no vices ask for their biological satisfaction, life does not please us any longer.

179. A psychoanalyst who applies therapy to students who want later to dedicate themselves to psychoanalytic research reports this case: "The man tried to get into theoretical discussion with me about various problems during his psychoanalysis. I was first surprised, but then I remembered what you had once told us in the seminar and repeated it to him. I said: 'I shall be delighted to discuss all these questions with you fully, but only after you have finished your therapeutic psychoanalysis. I'll invite you then to a cup of coffee and we shall talk about them. But only after you have finished your treatment, which will take a few months more.'"

180. Psychoanalyst to his patient at the end of the first interview: "I consider it a compliment to the intelligence of a man when you can be straightforward with him. Your analysis will not be easy, you will suffer during it, and it will stir you up. I can only promise you, as Churchill did to the British people, 'blood, sweat, and tears.' But at the end comes victory and the conquest of your emotional troubles."

181. A psychologist reports that a patient who has already gained much insight from his treatment told him: "Today I used a bus coming from Harlem when I came over. I was the only white person in the bus; all the other people were Negroes. When I sat there among all those colored people, I suddenly got very anxious for fear they might attack me. It was a feeling close to panic. It lasted only a few minutes, but the anxiety was very intense. When I got out of the bus I thought you would perhaps

interpret that upsurging anxiety as the result of an unconscious projection. You would perhaps say that I repressed intensively aggressive and violent impulses and projected them to the Negroes. It's quite possible, although I assure you nothing of this was felt by me."

182. Psychologist: "I often wonder whether those girls who cannot get along with their fathers and mothers and who escape from life in the family into marriage do not carry with them the conflict materials into their new menage."

"How strong is the lure of the forbidden! Look into dark hallways and park corners in the evenings and you will understand."

183. Old man: "It is not true that old age makes us childish. We remain childish all our life and old age makes it only more conspicuous by the contrast with biological senescence."

184. Woman during psychoanalytic session: "You know I had an afterthought just now. A thought such as comes up the stairs when all the guests are already present."

185. A patient: "Have I really to know myself? I thought only the other day that I would like to restrict the circle of my acquaintances. I really would rather skip myself and would prefer to remain a stranger to myself if only the others know me."

186. Older man: "Only young people are free and can go out into the world. We old people are imprisoned within ourselves, our old ideas and prejudices. There are no new potentialities for us and the inner world closes up on us as if it were a jail or, rather, a grave."

187. A psychiatrist explains: "There are only two short cuts to recovery from emotional disturbances: to fall in love with a person or to become enthusiastic for some-

thing like a cause or an idea. What a pity that also those
ways out end only at the same point where we had been a
short time ago."

"Therapy of emotional disturbances is to a great extent
a question of alternatives."

188. Young Jewish man: "The ancient Hebrews took
off their shoes when they entered sacred ground. Women
step out of their shoes whatever the ground may be. I
saw a woman sitting down at the dinner-table of a party
flinging off her shoes immediately and putting them on as
soon as she was ready ḭ ɡͼͳ ḽ ͼ ͻm the table."

189. *Memories from Old Vienna.* I often saw Catholic
nuns in the streets when I was a little boy and I thought at
first they were penguins, those funny birds I had seen in
my picture books. The nuns looked like them with their
long black gowns and that piece of white cloth on their
head. You saw almost no face.

Whenever it was discussed that a situation would have
been quite different if certain other things had only been
different, my father sometimes caricatured the nonsense
of such idle discussions, saying: "If Aunt Fanny had
wheels, she would be an omnibus."

190. Woman during her first psychoanalytic session:
"There is, I believe, a fly on this wall. I hope in your interest that it is not a bug."

191. Man: "Women have difficulty coming to the point.
They almost always start from the periphery and work to
the center. Perhaps it has some connection with their
curves."

"'Are you man or are you mouse?' my wife asked me
today when I told her I didn't dare to ask the boss for a
new raise. 'Mouse,' I answered, because I know she is
not afraid of any man, but she is afraid of even the
smallest mouse."

192. Supplementary remark on the origin of repression: If the process of repression originates in the world outside the child (parents and educators) and is then internalized, why is that origin so rarely remembered? The question is perhaps best solved by a comparison: the child is often admonished by his parents to look both right and left before crossing a street to avoid danger from approaching cars. Twenty years later the adult automatically does this and exercises caution before crossing the street. Only in exceptional cases will he remember that the now-habitual caution was induced by the warnings of mother or father.

193. A lawyer dreams that he appeals the case he lost the other day. In reality he does not intend to appeal. In the thought associations he reports after he has recounted the dream he speaks of the evening before the dream. He had been impotent with a woman he had taken home and to whom he felt attracted. The way to the interpretation of the dream is thus paved. Falling asleep, the lawyer planned to renew the sexual attempt and try again to regain his sexual potency with the woman. The dream distortion worked here in the displacement from the sexual area to the legal sphere. The thought connection is, of course, secured by the fact that he had recently lost that trial case.

194. Very old man paying compliments to the young, beautiful wife of a man in his early thirties, turns to this husband and says: "I wish I could still give you reasons for being jealous, Sir."

195. A repairman in an auto garage, a primitive person, who had not been able to finish high school, began an affair with a divorced woman who lived in the same house. This woman, a few years older than he, was a col-

lege professor and was superior to him not only socially but also with regard to education and background. The man, who had a certain intelligence, asked himself what the woman could see in him and what she found with him and not with other men. He finally became courageous enough to ask her directly about it. She simply answered: "I can relax with you."

196. Here is an extraordinary example of the expression rage can find in a woman. A patient, a middle-aged woman who lived with her husband on a lonely farm in New Mexico, once had a furious quarrel with him. While he later sat in his room writing letters, she went to his closet and took all his trousers and hid them in the cellar after having put them into a traveling box. Then she went to the stable, saddled her horse and rode around in the fields for a few hours. When she finally returned, her husband was in despair because he had had important business in the village and could not ride there without pants.

197. Young married woman: "I don't understand the casual way in which men speak about sexual intercourse with women in their past. 'Well,' says my husband, 'it was just a roll in the hay and didn't mean anything.' What would men say if we women felt the same way about sexual affairs with men?"

"If my husband would have sexual intercourse only when I really wished it, he would have only a few occasions on certain days every month."

"While my husband makes love to me, I sometimes think what I should cook tomorrow for dinner."

198. Girl telling her life story: "My mother died four years ago. We had a great argument in the morning but everything was all right in the evening. But she died the

next day of a heart attack and since then I cannot get rid of the thought that I am responsible for her death on account of that argument."

199. Psychologist: "Goethe before he wrote the *Suffering of Young Werther* and after it—those are two different persons. I often wondered why psychiatrists and psychologists concentrate on the preconditions of creativity and do not consider the psychotherapeutic effect of creative writing."

"I believe a writer has his material as a sculptor has, only it is not visible. It is in his mind. He works on that material as the sculptor on a figure he imagines. He cuts pieces away from it, adds a little, steps back and looks at it as if he were a stranger, an onlooker from outside."

200. Writer: "A fellow who can sit down with his friends in a restaurant and talk during a whole evening and even into the night describing the people in his office, how they are and what their relations to each other are, then speak at length about his wife and his kids, how they are, what they say and how they act—a fellow who does that evening after evening is perhaps an excellent conversationalist, but scarcely a good writer."

201. *Man a social animal:* No man and no woman can get along with others so long as they have not learned to live with themselves. But who are they themselves? To a great extent their personalities are results of the introjection of their parents or of other persons who had a decisive part in forming their personality in childhood.

Whoever cannot live with himself thus continues a conflict with those persons who had molded his infantile character. On this detour one arrives at the genetic conclusion: Whoever cannot live with himself must have had great difficulties in getting along with others.

202. *Relations with the psychoanalyst:* A sarcastic pa-

tient: "The physical handicap a psychoanalyst can most easily tolerate is deafness, since he does not listen anyhow."

"I brought you a very practical and appropriate Christmas gift—a nutcracker."

203. Man in his sixties: "I thought of Goethe's *Faust* yesterday before falling asleep. What old man would not sell his soul to the devil if there was the certainty that he would be young again?"

204. Young man who sometimes comes to psychoanalytic sessions after having enjoyed several dry martinis enters the consultation room: "Hi, Pop!"

205. Dream interpretation. A young man in whose psychoanalysis I could show that in his childhood he had been afraid that his father could castrate him, dreamed: "I attack my father with a knife and cut across his throat." The dream seems flagrantly to contradict my preceding statement, but this is valid only for its manifest content. Its interpretation entails a reversal of its latent content —which on one hand confirms my statement, on the other hand contains, so to speak, the corresponding action of the son against his father. The dream distortion becomes transparent when one follows the displacement from below to above, from the penis to the throat.

206. A Gentile patient: "There is no hostility any longer between Gentiles and Jews, only an uneasiness."

207. A middle-aged Jewish man: "Every Jewish father strives that his son should make a good living and every Jewish mother wants her daughter to be married to such a man."

208. Middle-aged man, remembering his childhood: "My mother told me that I should never put the knife with which I cut meat into my mouth. On Friday evening an old aunt was always with us at dinner. I liked to

tease her, especially about her table manners. She always put food on the knife and then ate from it. Once I asked her: 'Auntie, do you like sharp things?' I was scolded by mother later on for my impudence."

The same man about food preferences: "I like matzo-ball soup, especially when it is cooked with small pieces of ham."

Older Jewish man: "I agree with Freud that we don't need religion any longer in our civilization. Its function was also before our time not so much the belief in God, but rather the regulation of social intercourse."

The same man: "Christianity, Judaism, Islam is all the same to me. I have nothing against religion, but there should be no god in it."

209. Seminar student reporting a case: "The patient made long pauses in her first psychoanalytic sessions and when I asked her to tell me what she was thinking of, she said: 'I have a secret, and I cannot tell you about it.' I told her that she could talk about it later after she put more trust in me, but that it was of course impossible to keep a certain area reserved. I remembered then the comparison of Freud that Dr. Reik once told us here and I repeated it, asking her: 'Let's assume that in a city the police can enter every part of it except a certain quarter which is forbidden to the cops. Do you think that the security of the citizens in this territory could be insured?' "

210. Another student reporting a case: "The patient fell asleep in the middle of the sessions after he had already yawned and spoken in a very low voice. I let him take that nap and when he awoke, I told him that he had unconscious death-wishes against me which he acted out in demonstrating to me that I should die, go to eternal sleep."

211. In another seminar for psychoanalytic students,

the emotional development of a patient was discussed. It was pointed out that his present feminine and masochistic-passive attitude toward his father and to father-representative figures does not exclude that there was preceding it a childhood phase in which he had a strongly masculine and even a competitive attitude toward them. Under the deep-reaching influence of the castration-fear he yielded to father and got under the regime of the reversed Oedipus complex. This development is quite understandable if only one thinks in historical terms and compares the various layers of individual development to the different strata of ancient Troy as Heinrich Schliemann discovered and excavated it.

212. Patient after a psychoanalytic interpretation: "If I understand you properly, you consider childhood as a kind of kindergarten for the love life of man?"

213. A student who is depressed reports: "I asked that old professor of philosophy whom I accompanied home after his lecture if there is a formula for being happy. He smiled and said: 'I doubt it.' But I insisted and asked him if there is at least a formula to become less unhappy. He looked at me and said: 'Perhaps if you can prevent men from becoming old.' But I am young and I am unhappy. 'Oh,' he said, 'that will pass. The main thing is to remain healthy.' You see how he shifted from one opinion to the other?"

The same young man, same session: "I believe that women in general are less unhappy than men. That is because they treat things not as seriously as men. They do not consider the same things as seriously as we, have no principles and don't give a damn about laws and orthography. Even financial misery does not frighten them. They can be very sad one moment and laugh aloud the next. They are so much nearer emotionally to children."

214. Psychologist: "I am doing Rohrschach, free association tests, and such things at the clinic. To tell the truth, I have no great trust in all those tests. A little story I heard the other day is pertinent: A psychiatrist who has a first interview with a patient puts two small pencil dots close together on a piece of paper. He shows it to the patient and asks him what he sees there. The patient answers: 'Two fleas having sexual intercourse.' The psychiatrist takes the paper back, enlarges the size of dots, and shows it again to the patient, asking him the same question. The patient now answers: 'Those are two flies having sexual intercourse.' The psychiatrist thinks this over and says to the patient: 'You know that you have a sexual problem.' The patient says: 'Yeah, but you're not helping me by showing me all those dirty pictures.'"

215. Anger need not be repressed in order to become emotionally harmful. It may be only denied or disavowed by a person for a longer time or it may accumulate. Whatever the reasons for its nonexpression, intense anger or spite will find hidden channels to make its presence known. The best condition for observing reactions of this kind is in married life, in which annoyance denied by wife or husband finds voice at a remote place or at a situation whose character or circumstances are quite different from the original one.

What results from those observations with regard to practical wisdom as well as mental hygiene? It is often impossible to express intense annoyance because it would hurt the feelings of a person one loves, because the social situation forbids such a manifestation, or for various other reasons. Disavowal or denial of such strong feelings can be emotionally harmful and find a replaced tumultuous and apparently unjustified expression, especially in the case of accumulation.

The best psychological advice is to avoid as much as possible repression, denial, and disavowal so that the feelings of annoyance or anger are conscious to the person who exercises restraint or control, especially when the situation demands it.

216. Old man in first interview: "I have had this claustrophobia since I was twenty years old . . . I am now sixty-two. I always get panicky on an escalator. How long would it take you to cure this?"

217. Man in psychoanalytic treatment: "When I was a little boy, I was ashamed because my parents were divorced and I thought I must have been a bad boy."

218. *Childhood memory:* A patient remembers that his father took him to the golf course the first time when he was six years old. When their car was near the golf course, the father showed the boy a building into which he should go to fetch the clubs and the ball. The boy was very willing to get them, but what astonished him was the manner in which he should ask for them. "Tell the man there that you want the sticks and ball for Mr. Edward Glanzl." The boy wondered why his father found it necessary to tell him his name as if the child did not know it.

219. The strange childhood memory of a woman patient puzzled me for a long time. The girl, daughter of an East European rabbi, did not feel any strong feelings of mourning or grief when her father died. She was ten years old then and she admired and loved her father very much. Not only was the absence of any mourning for him conspicuous, even more surprising was a feeling of satisfaction that he had died, an emotion she clearly remembered as having experienced at the time but for which she had no explanation. The solution of that psychological mystery came much later during the psychoanalytical treatment—its nature had to be concluded from other

childhood memories emerging in another context. A few years before her father's death a scholar she often heard discuss Talmudic problems with her father came several times to their house when her father was absent. This man, a few years younger than her father, but also highly respected, used the absence of the master of the house to play sexually with the girl. The child was very much ashamed, but dared neither reject him nor tell her father. Her greatest worry, increasing with time, was that her father could find out about those disgraceful sexual incidents. Her rising anxiety at the thought of such a possibility led finally to the unconscious idea that her father could die before he knew about those scenes. This thought-connection explains the absence of mourning for the loved man as well as the emergence of the strange satisfaction after his death.

220. *On the psychology of women:* A woman who is often proud of being different from other women, either in the mode of her life (profession, bachelor girl, whore, or nun) or in a special social situation, will in spite of all sometimes have moods in which she wants to be like other women whom she need not even envy at other times. She may then wish to have the pleasures and sorrows of other women, to share their lot even when she despised them before. It is not so much conformity or compliance as it is the desire to share the ordinary lot of all women and not be excluded from their community.

221. Patient about a psychoanalyst he knows: "Some people are quite good in solving other people's problems, but are helpless with their own."

222. Older man: "What is religion after all? An attempt at consolation for us who will die."

223. A neurotic patient reports: "I experience a special pleasure when I see a young woman putting on gloves,

especially narrow white ones. I observe her movements, how she slips them on so that they fit tightly and don't make creases." The psychoanalytic interpretation of that symptomatic liking arrives at the conclusion that here a transference from below to above has taken place. Unconsciously the patient identified the hand with the penis and the glove with the female genitals. The symbolism thus leads to the interpretation: the woman herself puts the penis into the vagina and fits it in.

224. *Beethoven:* Bismarck said that he would feel always courageous if he could hear Beethoven's symphonies daily. That was a hundred years ago. Today statesmen can hear Beethoven's symphonies not only daily but as often as they wish—thanks to modern devices. But no emotional improvements have been observed in statesmen as a result.

225. A writer who reads over what he has written a long time ago is generally dissatisfied with it and sometimes does not even recognize the writings as his own. His experience may be similar to that of Toscanini who, on a voyage by steamer, once heard a recording of Beethoven's "Eroica," was very annoyed by the reproduction and found it highly unsatisfactory. He was finally told that it was the record of his own conducting of the symphony.

226. High school teacher: "I had a dream. In it I had to give some mathematical tests only to women. My mother and sister were among them. They were multiplications. . . . Oh, that's the old horseshit! Multiplication, women multiplaying, reproducing."

227. *Mathematical problem:* A patient who often looked at the newspaper of a neighbor on the bus or subway once read his own name, to his great astonishment. (The announcement of a book of his just published.) The patient occupied himself then with the question: what—

174 Voices from the Inaudible

according to the theory of probability—is the chance that an over-the-shoulder reader finds his name in a newspaper read by a stranger in a bus or in a subway—especially when the furtive reader is no celebrity?

228. Young man: "We sat on a bench in Central Park, my friends and I, and discussed women and experiences in sex. On the neighboring bench sat a very old man. He could not help hearing what we said. I looked furtively at him from time to time. He did not even smile at our chatter. He just looked sad. I would have liked to go over to him and ask him what he thought about love and sex."

229. Psychologists working on a thesis on the psychology of old age: "It is remarkable that the circle of interests shrinks much more and rapidly in an old man than in an old woman."

230. Man returning from summer vacation: "There was tomato soup on the menu of the hotel (which was run by Quakers), and I said to the waiter: 'Tomato soup is an abomination to the Lord.'"

About a woman: "She said 'I've got my pride,' but she forgets it sometimes."

231. Young man: "'Don't be an ass,' I said to my friend, but I know that this admonition was a futile one. He is not exactly an ass, but a mule and just as incorrigibly stubborn as a mule."

232. There are certain characteristic features common to people who have the same profession—writers, lawyers, physicians, carpenters, waiters. It seems the same profession develops certain manners and mannerisms in the people who share it and stamps them sometimes beyond nation and religion. Even the professional quality has different nuances and shades. Think of the friendliness of your grocer who greets you as a customer, of the inviting kindness of a lawyer whose client you will be, and of the

dignified friendliness of the physician opening the door of his consultation room and calling you in.

233. Psychologist in training analysis: "Today I saw in a bus an advertisement for CARE packages. There was the picture of a boy and the slogan 'Hunger can't wait.' I had just come from a lecture on the theory of sublimation and I asked myself 'Can sex wait?' The theory concerns libidinous feelings like desire or love that can be sublimated, but purely physical sensations—'sexual arousal'—cannot be sublimated There is not time for it. You can postpone pissing for a short tim., but when the drive gets imperative, then you have to let go. Sexuality in its crude and original form can wait as little as hunger. A man who tries to 'sublimate' when sexually aroused will not be surprised when he feels that he approaches an emission of ejaculation and also a woman will feel how she is lubricating and experience an orgasm, whatever this may be in women."

"Yesterday I saw in *The New York Times* an advertisement for the Berlitz school: a little Negro boy and the caption 'He speaks Ewe. Do you?' I thought of a discussion we recently had about the strange kinds of communication women have when they are in the company of men. We don't understand this kind of mutual understanding. It is as if it moves in a different groove and when women talk together it often is as if they speak in an untranslatable foreign, or even exotic, language like Ewe. In the discussion we had circled around the question of whether this kind of communication is connected with their femaleness or whether an old tradition among women is carried on from one generation to the next. On second thought I came to the conclusion that there is no irreconcilable contradiction there, because that little Negro boy also learns to speak Ewe from his parents and especially from his mother, who spoke to him all the time when he was a baby."

234. *The boss.* "Today my boss lost patience with me and shouted: 'Go to hell!' and I answered: 'I have been there for a long time. It's the sixth year that I've been in this office of yours, *Sir.*'"

235. *The suitcase.* With few exceptions, women pack their suitcases carefully. When you open the suitcase of a woman and see it crammed with things in a very disorderly manner—lingerie, dresses, and shoes pushed carelessly one on top of the other, you will arrive at three possibilities: either the woman is a schizophrenic or she was blindly hurried or she was thrown into an extraordinary emotional turmoil, engaged in violent commotion. If you can exclude the possibility of schizophrenia, the most likely assumption is that of great agitation, because only very excited women are in a hurry.

236. *The same dress.* Two of the most elegant women of Vienna came to blows in the salon of M—not, as you might assume, in jealous rivalry over a man, but over a dress. Both had come back recently from Paris and had bought the same dress. They ran into each other during a party, each in the identical model. In the salon, one was dramatically confronted by the other. The scene blazed then into a flagrant scandal.

237. *After the operation.* "No," said the nurse to the visitor, "I have not yet taken this patient's temperature, but I know she is much better. When she woke up this morning, the first thing she asked for was her lipstick and the second her new bed jacket."

238. *The magic carpet.* Are there times of departure for magic carpets? Or can everyone take off when he wants to? If there is a timetable and you miss one magic carpet,

can you take the next one? What is the fare for the trip?
Is it only the loss of the sense of reality?

239. *The I.* Quite a few psychological problems of individuals and of groups would be made approachable if
one considered that the *We* is so much older than the *I*.
When one wants to measure the interval between the mass
and the emergence of the individual, one will best compare the time when the child becomes first aware that he
is a separate individual and says *I*. Before this time the
child speaks of himself in the third person ("Charlie,"
"Joan"). The child thus at first looks on himself as others
look on him and does not conceive of himself as a separate
being.

240. *Self-hate.* Women would not easily admit it, but
they sometimes hate themselves after their husband or
lover has reproached them for something they did wrong
or omitted to do. Such self-hate often emerges after the
man has left and they are alone with themselves.

241. *Marital interlude.* "I nagged him, it's true, the
whole morning, but he read the newspaper and did not
pay any attention to me. He then put the newspaper aside
and said only 'Crawl down from me, would you?' "

242. *Sexual prelude.* When you consider the psychological significance and repercussions of sexual play in
which everything but intercourse itself takes place you
will wonder about the circumlocutory phrases we are using. Don't we speak of "heavy petting"?

243. *Man and marriage.* "It is not enough for my wife
that I hear her talking all the time—'blah blah blah.' She
also expects that I should listen to what she is saying."

244. *Women about women.* "You ask me how I know
that my friends say terrible things about me when
I am not there? That's very simple. Because I too say atro-

cious things about each of them when she is not present.
Gossip is a two-way street. . . . You know I believe that
there is gossip even in heaven; I am sure, at least, among
the female angels there."

245. *Education.* The art and science of education is fascinated by the problems children have and occupies itself
with the question how best to grapple with those problems. It seems to me that pedagogy neglects in this one-
sidedness the personality of the educator. How to educate a child depends not only on the kind of child one has
to deal with but also on the kind of pedagogue who under-
takes the task. In other words: "Pedagogue, educate yourself!"

246. *On narcissism.* There is a certain kind of displaced
and generalized narcissism that does not restrict itself to
the person himself. There are, for instance, many women
who are so much in love with themselves and so vainglori-
ous that they are profoundly convinced that they have the
most beautiful and gifted children in the world, the best
husbands, the nicest apartments, and even the kindest
mothers-in-law.

247. *Fragment of a teasing dialogue.* "Well, I made the
girl pregnant, so . . ."

"You made the girl pregnant, you say? I didn't know
you had it in you."

248. *Girl about young men.* "Either they do it or they
make a pass at you because they want to do it or they at
least think of doing it. I sometimes wonder whether they
think of anything else when they are with a young
woman."

249. *Courage.* It takes guts to do what you really want
to do. More than that: it takes guts to think through what
you really want to do.

250. *A conspiracy of the professions.* Bernard Shaw had

one of the characters in *The Doctor's Dilemma* say: "All professions are conspiracies against the laity." He could have added that one of the best protective measures against the intrusion of laymen is the professional jargon, the more or less scientific terminology. Some lawyers, physicians, and psychoanalysts have perfected that professional jargon with such a degree of virtuosity that not even other lawyers, physicians, and psychoanalysts are able to grasp the meaning of their papers or speeches.

251. *Unconscious resistance to marriage.* Two cases of women recently treated showed a surprising resemblance in their unconscious resistance to marriage. The younger woman had relations with eligible bachelors who liked her and frequently took her out. When the relationship with those men reached a certain degree of intimacy or affection, she always experienced an increasing anxiety that she would lose the man or he would desert her. He always did. Either he did not appear any more or explained to her that he could not marry her for this or that reason. It became clear soon that she unconsciously managed this outcome. Her anxiety was, so to speak, the anticipated unconscious wish with a negative sign.

The older woman always glided into platonic friendships with men who turned out to be inappropriate love objects. They were mostly married, fathers of several children and unwilling to get divorced to marry her.

In both cases the women had a fixation on their mothers and their resistance to a possible marriage which they consciously desired was determined to a great extent by their unconscious decisions to stay with their mothers.

252. *Apology and repetition.* A gifted student observed that a person can apologize so sincerely and so profusely, yet later repeats the act for which he has apologized in the first place.

The observation is certainly accurate for a majority of cases. The student expressed the opinion that the succession apology-deed works perhaps the same as the repetition-compulsion. This interpretation cannot be correct or complete because it does not consider the part words play in that succession. Apologies are expressed in words that make, so to speak, the act undone and make a clean sweep of the surface so that forbidden impulses can re-emerge.

253. *Other memories of Old Vienna.* A patient reports that his older brother had a special manner of making a fool of his wife. There was in Vienna after the first war an humanitarian enterprise to help the poorest and the needy, called *Winterhilfe* (Winterhelp). A collector came to the door to collect money for that specific charity. The brother of the patient, a civil servant, received the collector very courteously and shouted to his wife: "Louise, wonderful news! We are rescued. Winterhelp is here."

Another manner of teasing his wife was to pretend that she was deaf. The couple went, for instance, to a movie and the husband, bending to his wife's ear, shouted: "Many people here!" or "The house is full." He made his wife—who had excellent hearing—very embarrassed, especially when he continued the hoax.

On similar occasions, for instance attending a theater performance, he was unwilling to leave his cane at the cloakroom (also to save money). He then pretended to be lame on one foot and he had to lean upon the cane. He limped thus through the hall of the theater resting on his cane while his wife blushed in acute embarrassment.

254. *Memory of the past self.* It is relatively easy to remember the past so long as one's self is not present in it,

but it is often highly difficult to recreate one's own past self, to feel as reality how you used to be, what motivated your actions and your experiences. Your past life is a dream—sometimes even an anxiety-dream—and you are the most shadowy figure in it.

255. *Talkativeness.* There are a number of women who are so shy in company that they have to talk all the time to conceal it.

256. *The garlic neurosis.* A psychiatrist: "I call cases of that type garlic neurosis. The person who has eaten garlic does not feel bad, he only makes the others who surround him feel bad. Similarly, some neurotics are not crazy; they only drive all other people around them crazy."

257. *Hands in woman's view.* "Women's hands touching you never feel unpleasant. Men's hands are either wonderful when you want to be touched by them or horrible when you don't want them to touch you."

258. *On the psychology of procrastination.* Procrastination met either as neurotic symptom or as character trait in psychoanalytic treatment has not yet been given the psychological attention it deserves. The general motives of such trends, the delay and postponement, are obvious enough. A conscious or unconscious counter-will works against finishing a certain task or job. It is remarkable that this counter-tendency effects its purpose also in cases in which the person is consciously eager to do his work, even when he seems enthusiastic for it.

If the tendency of procrastination becomes very powerful, it enforces finally the abandonment of the work. One is entitled to conclude from this the unconscious purpose of the psychological attitude.

Special interest should be given those cases in which procrastination is tied to a certain event or the fulfillment of a definite condition. Also this thought-connection may occasionally become conscious and be immediately submerged, but remains in the majority of observed cases unconscious and has to be found by the psychoanalyst.

Here is a good example of such a case in which the procrastination became extreme and in which the secret condition on which it depended was discovered. A forty-year-old woman lived with her aged mother, who made great demands on her. The woman had remained single and ambitiously pursued an academic career. The old mother became ill and she had to have a difficult operation. While the daughter waited in Mother's room in the hospital, she did not doubt that any moment a nurse or a doctor would appear and announce that the mother had died on the operating table. Contrary to expectation, Mother was in good condition when she returned and recovered quickly. It was not difficult to guess what the thoughts of the daughter waiting for the outcome of the operation were: they had the earmarks of an unconscious death-wish.

The daughter had made a contract with a publisher to write a scientific book. It was only natural that she procrastinated at the time when she was worried about mother's bad health, but it was conspicuous that she could not work on the book following her mother's recovery. It finally became obvious that the procrastination had become a writer's block and she would be unable to finish the book by the deadline specified in the contract. Putting aside for the moment other psychological factors, the condition that had to be fulfilled before the book could be written became recognizable in psychoanalytic treatment. It was as if the daughter had made the unconscious decision: "I shall work on and finish the book only when mother dies." The part of self-sabotaging and self-punishing tendencies in the effect does not exclude the fact that the unconscious death-wishes against mother remained in this unconscious formulation victorious.

Also in other cases of such "time"-tied procrastination, the condition on which they depend is frequently the unconscious expectation that one of the persons near and dear to the subject should die.

259. *Identification with the male.* Unconscious identification of women with a man is sometimes expressed in a surprising fashion. Here are two examples of such manifestations from clinical experience: A high school teacher, a very intelligent and educated woman, was promiscuous. In a psychoanalytic session she once expressed the fear that she could become suddenly impotent. She knew, of course, the word *frigid.* The use of the word *impotent* was determined by unconscious identification with the male. Another patient, a medical student, went horseback riding only when she menstruated. It was as if the denial of the feminine role and the protest against it found unconscious expression in this symptomatic action.

260. *Latent homosexuality.* Unfounded and even delusional jealousy of a woman as well as contemptuous and hostile treatment of her are unmistakable indications of latent homosexual trends.

261. *The moralist and the psychologist.* The moralist sees only two colors in human nature: black and white. The psychologist has not such color-blindness. He is able to recognize the gray and the other color nuances and shades. More than this, he should be able to see the white spots in the black and the black in the white in human nature.

262. *That man.* Fred prefers young girls who are virgins; he likes to deflower them. The other day a friend of his said: "Wherever Fred goes, he leaves a trail of bloody girls behind him."

263. *A query.* I was asked: "Why do you quote more women than men discussing their spouses?" "Because women have more to say or rather to talk about. Beyond that, women are better at dialogue and much better in monologue than men."

264. *Corpulent men.* Young girl: "My girl friend has developed a passion for matchmaking and introduced a lawyer to me. He is rich, very intelligent, and only a few years older than I. A very eligible bachelor. What a pity that he is very paunchy. You know, I have a prejudice against corpulent men. I like them as uncles, lawyers, or such. But when I think of marrying a young man with a paunch, I immediately suspect that he could be impotent. You know what people say: 'A good cock does not get fat.'"

265. *Surprised by the unconscious.* At an informal gathering of relatives and friends, a man appeared with his little daughter. The shy little girl was clinging affectionately to her father. The hostess, playfully teasing the child, said to her: "Your daddy is not going home with you. He stays here for the night. He will not go to sleep with you, he will sleep with me." She became suddenly aware of what she had said and reddened with blushes.

266. *The ultimate reality.* The only reality from which we cannot divorce—either by religion or by any other illusion—and which we have to face is that we must die. Nothing in the world is so certain and so important.

It is now more than 175 years since Benjamin Franklin wrote in a letter that "in this world nothing can be said to be certain, except death and taxes." But death is, so to speak, more certain because it can take a man by surprise, while he must fill out his tax declaration. No one is too busy to die.

267. *Necessary lie.* "What do you say? I must not lie to my wife. But if I told her the truth all day long I would always arrive late at trains and airplanes, concerts and parties."

268. *Movies.* When you take a long walk in the streets of New York and look at the titles and the pictures on the marquees of houses, you will not doubt that psychoanalysis is correct in its main assumptions. What do you see announced there? Sex and murder.

269. *Cast down eyes.* It is now considered old-fashioned, but I still remember a time when married women as well as girls cast their eyes down when men looked at them. It was obvious that such looking had the meaning of wooing or sexual desire. Casting down of eyes on the side of the woman takes this for granted and reacts with a movement of shame or modesty. To cast a frank glance upon the man would in those past times have been considered an invitation or at least an acceptance of the man's invitation expressed by his looking at the woman.

270. *Fur coats.* Not even feminine fashions change so much as we imagine. The women of prehistoric ages covered themselves with the furs of the beasts their men had killed, of bears and tigers and so on. And the women of our time do the same. Even the psychological connection is almost uninterrupted. The women of that prehistoric past, wrapped in leopard furs, displayed what a powerful hunter her husband was, while the woman of our time shows that her husband or lover is a successful money-maker. The minks in which she is dressed are for her just such a status symbol as were the furs for the prehistoric female.

271. *Permanence.* The thought of permanence in their relationship is rarely absent in a woman's mind when she

enters a sexual affair with a man. The thought of having a baby with a woman with whom he has sexual relations is rarely present in a man's mind.

272. *A Haunting Melody.* October 1963: Edith Piaf is dead! A favorite chanson of hers, *La Vie en Rose*, begins to haunt me and I cannot get rid of the tender tune by Louigny or of the lines:

> *Quand il me prends dans ses bras,*
> *Il me parle tout bas*
> *Je vois la vie en rose.*
> *Il me dit des mots d'amour,*
> *Mots de tout de jour*
> *Et ca m'a fait quelque chose.*

Freely to translate:

> He speaks quite low,
> When he has his arms around me
> But life suddenly is wonderful to see.
> He tells me words of love
> Everyday words they'll be
> But they do something to me.

How stupid we were as young men who did not know that women are wooed and won by words! Second thought: Women can find those words much quicker and say them better than men can, but they rarely say them and prefer to hear them said by us, perhaps because it is more difficult for us men.

273. *Guilt feeling and self-punishment.* Freud frequently stated that conscious guilt feelings and self-punishment can scarcely coexist. He once gave the following instance: a man who stole $100,000 and escaped to South America where he enjoys his affluence, may (assumed as a theoretical possibility) sometimes feel guilty.

But when the man who stole the money, in leaving the place of his deed, breaks his leg, he may not feel guilty because he feels he has already punished himself.

When one becomes old, our misdeeds and the hurts and harms we inflicted on others reappear in quieter hours and sleepless nights, as Banquo's ghost appears to Macbeth. They seem to accumulate; always new ones emerge. ("What—will the line stretch out to the crack of doom?" cries Macbeth.) Yet this does not prevent us afterwards from doing wrong and hurting people's feelings.

To draw a balance sheet of one's life amounts almost to a confession.

274. *Self-conception of women.* Widows and women whose husbands have left them feel after some time a very distinct loss of their social esteem and soon also a diminution of their self-esteem. This is especially conspicuous when their husband had an important job or a well-known social function.

275. *Beauty and suffering.* One must suffer to be beautiful (*Il faut sufrir pour être belle*). At least one thing men need not worry about in addition to taxes, communism, unemployment and so on.

276. *Respect for women.* There is a single place where high respect and delicate consideration for women is, from a certain moment on, ill-timed: in bed. Women begin to hate it when men then treat them respectfully instead of being violently passionate.

277. *Small talk.* Women who have no small talk are either neurotic or enviously step aside for another woman who has, or are in general revolt against the feminine role.

278. *Knowing women.* Women are known to us mostly by direct or indirect observations of men and by occasional remarks of other women. The first source is, of course, utterly unreliable and the second insufficient because it is

not only prejudiced and distorted, but also only trickling and scarce. Not only the feminine restraint in expression, but also solidarity among women interferes with the clarity of statements.

How do we know women? I repeat: Mostly by information from men. The best we can recognize about their nature is conveyed to us by gynecologists—mostly men too.

279. *The other woman.* A man may often imagine what made another man act this way or the other and frequently guesses right. But a woman knows, so to speak, instinctively or intuitively how another woman would act in this or that situation and is rarely wrong in her assumptions. They include not only good intentions, but malicious designs and disastrous schemes.

280. *Emotional loneliness.* Young woman: "I can stand physical loneliness quite well, but emotional loneliness not at all. When I know that there is no one who cares for me, when I don't love anyone, I became gloomily depressed and even desperate."

281. *Two-sided sword.* A college student did not like one of his teachers who favored other pupils. The young man made himself particularly objectionable with that teacher and failed in his course. He had expressed his aggression against the professor, but simultaneously sabotaged himself.

282. *A strange comparison.* A young woman speaking about another one: "Do you know the new doors in supermarkets and department stores marked *Out?* When you approach them, they open themselves—you never even touch the door-latch—and you are already out. That's exactly the manner in which that woman let the man get away from her. He made perhaps once a slighting remark

and she let him leave. She must be either very proud or she has a better man she wants to marry."

283. *An organic sensation.* A young woman, speaking of her boy friend: "He is a toucher and I often put out a 'Don't touch' sign." After a pause: "I hear the clock tick—that's the first time for months."

It was easy to guess that the ticking of the clock was a displacement of a clitoris-sensation, awakened by the memory of her boy friend's touching her and of her sexual excitement.

284. *Emancipation of women.* Physician at a party: "A man really needs several women. A housewife, a helpmate, a woman for his bed."

An older man asks: "You mean, a kind of unofficial harem? But how is it when the woman arrogates the same rights and says she needs several men?" "Oh, that's different."

285. *The missed part.* A little girl who was allowed to look at television every evening before going to bed was taken to a movie the first time. On the way home she asked: "Mama, where were the commercials?"

286. *Women's solidarity.* Women's solidarity, confronted by men, is a special case of those who are or think they are handicapped and must defend themselves on account of their weaknesses.

The acceptance of gallantry displayed to women appears to be a tacit acknowledgment of those originally anatomical handicaps. A rejection of gallantry would thus psychologically amount to their indignant denial or deliberate disavowal.

287. *Children and adults.* Look at the expressions of joy of little boys and girls, their eyes, their legs, their arms! The pleasure of us grown-ups, our mirth, is only a

diluted and anemic second edition of the jubilation of those young children.

288. *Reading certain novels.* Is it true that with advanced age men lose the taste for reading novels? I, at least, often become bored with long-winded descriptions of certain characters in works of fiction. I feel then as if I were visiting someone who shows you the family-album explaining to you that was Auntie Jenny and that Cousin Alfred. They are convinced that you are as much interested in them as they are.

289. *Beauty and old age.* Shakespeare's line "Age cannot wither her . . ." is rather an expression of wishful thinking than the statement of a reality. Cleopatra would in her old age have shriveled up, perhaps full of wrinkles; her gait would be far different from the graciousness of her youth, and as an old woman she would drag herself miserably from one place to another.

290. *The talkative sex.* I wonder why no one has called women "the talkative sex." Women can indeed be silent in company of men, but to remain silent when they are among women only is an endurance test for them.

291. *Tears and laughter.* Men are often astonished at how easily women weep and laugh, but men do not consider that the crying or laughing of women can be purposely produced to attain certain effects, or that the woman does not necessarily feel the corresponding emotions. Few men, actors among them, can do that.

292. *In retrospect.* Older Frenchman remembering: "How beautiful and peaceful was married life at the period when every husband had a legitimate mistress."

293. *The fine art of cooking.* "My wife cannot cook. I imagine even a healthy dog would get stomachaches after having eaten what she cooked."

294. *Age and speed.* Young boys and girls almost al-

ways run, although they have so many decades of living before them, while old people whose lifetime is limited always walk slowly.

295. *At home and abroad.* Psychoanalysts often hear that women and men behave differently at home and when they are abroad, especially in a sexual direction. Many people who are almost puritanical in America feel that they can indulge their inclinations when they are in France or Spain. In some cases you get the impression that the local distance replaces another one—the suspension of authoritarian forbiddings.

296. *Narcissistic character.* The narcissistic character of a woman patient revealed itself in many directions. She started her psychoanalytic session with the sentence: "Today I have nothing to say. Therefore I dressed very carefully so that at least I look pretty." The day before she had said to her boy friend: "I am not one of the fifty girls with whom you go around. I am something special and when you do not realize that I don't want to see you any longer."

297. *Paradoxical behavior.* A woman almost immediately made herself objectionable whenever her husband or another man showed consideration for her. She was suspicious that this was done because she was "only a woman." Such paradoxical behavior became especially conspicuous when she had her monthly period.

298. Future pedagogy will pay more attention than now to the attitude of father to daughter. In certain social or religious circles a boy is valued higher by his father than is the daughter, even when she is superior to her brother in intelligence and character. This was the case also with the girl I just mentioned. She grew up in an orthodox Jewish milieu in which a boy as "the Kaddish" is favored. She remembered that she was very well aware that she was more intelligent than the younger brother her father pre-

ferred to her. As a little girl she indignantly asked her father: "Why can he," pointing to the brother, "become a rabbi and not I?"

299. *Heaven.* How poor and beggarly were our conceptions of heaven when we were children, compared with the ideas of modern children! I heard an eight-year-old girl ask her mother: "But is there no telephone and television in heaven?"

300. *Imprints in language.* The archaic language of symbolism does not appear only in the formation of dreams. It has also left indelible traces in everyday language. Psychoanalysis teaches us that the fear of falling from a height can be recognized as unconscious repression of yielding to an erotic temptation. But do we not (or rather did we not) speak of "fallen women"? Many clinical experiences taught us that people who have a passionate interest in fires are extremely ambitious characters. Our language knows the expression "burning ambition." Psychoanalytic experiences convinced us that among the character traits of analerotic persons parsimoniousness, even avarice, has a prominent place. The retaining of feces is unconsciously connected with stinginess. The word *close* —still used, as in "a close man"—points in the same direction; it has the connotation of niggardliness, penuriousness, or stinginess.

301. *Mozart.* Leaving a concert of Mozart's works together, an acquaintance and I became engaged in a debate about the personality of the composer. The man quoted letters of Mozart and other contemporary documents to prove to me that the composer was a very envious and malicious person, a character quite different from the naïve and kind personality as which he often appears in the biographies. "Did he murder people?" I asked, "I mean, murder not in thoughts (we all do that)

but in material reality? Did he steal anything other than a few tunes which he transformed in such a way that he made them his own?" I asked.

But even if he did, how much terrible evil could he effect in a life time that lasted not even thirty-six years? Even if he did all the evils of the world in this time, I couldn't care less. He has atoned for it for giving pure delight to human beings for more than two hundred years and every priest in the world would tell him: "*Absolvo te.*" If there is anything in the Catholic concept of heaven, Mozart is now one of the favored angels of God and when this angel sits down and begins to play one of his concertos, the Lord is delighted and smiles.

302. *Relativity of values.* When you are dressed in a jacket, have a black tie on, and kill a few people, you are called a mass-murderer and eventually suffer the death penalty. When you have an earth-colored uniform on doing the same things you are an ardent patriot and, if the enemy kills you, you die a laureled hero.

If you are a woman, you may dress as a man at your convenience and take a walk. If you are a man and dress as a woman, the police will arrest you when you appear on the street.

If you are a man and an early-morning visitor arrives, you will not be too embarrassed by the state of your apartment. A woman would feel that she must offer apologies for the disorder.

As a man, if you pay much attention to what people say about your appearance, you will be considered effeminate. As a woman who appears not to care what people say about your looks, dresses, and so on, you will be considered unfeminine.

Assume you are a young man and have the genius of Einstein or Freud and you pass on the street a young woman you don't know but to whom you feel attracted. Will she smile at you? Never.

Assume you are a small child just able to walk, insignificant, equally unknown to the woman who passes you on the street. Will she smile at you? Certainly.

303. *The Last Mahler* (a supplement to *The Haunting Melody*). We know a great deal about the dynamics responsible for the process of repression but we know little about the emotional agents that bring repressed material back to the surface. Here is an excellent example of this kind.

My book *The Haunting Melody,* the major part of which deals with Gustav Mahler, was written in 1952 and published by Farrar, Straus in 1953. A few days ago (which means more than eleven years later) a memory concerning the composer emerged with full clarity. I could take an oath upon it that it had never occurred to me in those eleven years.

I can at least guess what brought the long-buried memory back. We, my son and my grandson who studies music and I, had just come from a performance of Mahler's Ninth Symphony. Descending the stairs of Carnegie Hall I said to my son that I consider the first movement of that symphony the greatest music Mahler composed and that he had finally found himself there. We stood then at the street corner near Carnegie Hall waiting for a taxi to take us home. A late cab drove by. Has this to do with the reemergence of the memory? Perhaps.

Here is that memory. It must have been about 1916 or 1917 in Vienna—I was in uniform but not yet a lieutenant —and we had come from a party at Heinrich Grünbaum's. The Grünbaums lived near the Karlskirche in the fourth district of Vienna. A doctor and I walked to the Ringstrasse, talking about all kinds of things. I don't know any longer how and why he began to tell me about Gustav Mahler. The doctor had been the official physician of the Vienna Opera while Mahler was its director (1897 on). I shall say a few words about why I forgot his name later, but first here is what he told me.

Director Mahler once took one of the pretty ballerinas with him when he drove home in a cab from a performance at the opera. There was some petting and embracing during the drive. Suddenly Mahler was put into a black humor and left the cab. The next day Mahler told the physician that the girl put her tongue into his mouth, and he seriously asked whether this was a sexual perversion.

I smiled, of course, at Mahler's naïveté (he must have been then thirty-eight or thirty-nine years old), but I felt somehow embarrassed, as if the doctor had committed an indiscretion toward his patient. I know this sounds ridiculous—Mahler had died five or six years before—but I was then a severe moralist, had finished my psycho-analytic training with Dr. Karl Abraham a short time before and must have felt that the physician had somehow exposed Mahler, whom I worshiped at the time. It must have been this silly reason which made me forget the name of the doctor (a name easily to be found in Vienna).

The deep impression made by the first movement of the Ninth Symphony awakened other decisive impressions. It made me think of the contrast between the young Mahler and the middle-aged composer who wrote the Ninth Symphony in 1910. It was his last work and he must have known sometimes that he would not live long, although he often in other moods thought that he would reach an old age.

In the center of my train of thoughts was the idea of death as it appeared to the young composer, the man to whom his physician had said in 1907 that his heart was not in good condition. What an emotional and mental difference between those two situations! The thought of death is close to the young composer of the *Kindertotenlieder* as well as of many early songs. It is there in the first symphonies. It is rarely missing in the later ones, but even then in 1907 it is there, so to speak, as an abstract idea, not as frightening reality. But when he was told in the summer of 1907 about his heart condition, he became anxious and cautious. His wife reported that this mood of resignation was in his last years replaced by a terrible hunger for life and a tremendous fear of dying.

There was no flirtation any more with the German Volkslied, no sentimentality connected with the idea of immortality, only the confrontation with the thought of death. The *Lied von der Erde,* especially "Der Abschied," and the first movement of the Ninth Symphony speak most eloquently of that mood.

Why did that old memory of the episode with the ballerina re-emerge after the performance of the Ninth Symphony? It must be that I thought of the contrast of the young director who was a puritan and Mahler after 1907 who had (especially after his long consultation with Freud in Leiden) again approached his wife sexually, something he had not done for years. Now he realized that he had "lived wrongly" as he said. Now he recognized that this is the only world at our disposal; beyond it is only the grave. Alas, not much more time was allotted to him. That consultation with Freud took place in August 1910. Eight months later Mahler was dead. But in the last unfinished symphony on which he worked, between the lines of that Tenth Symphony there were passionate outcries. The sketch of the finale has the line "To live for thee! To die for thee! Almshi!"

He embraced the beauty of woman and of earth only a

very short time, but only because death made him drop his arms.

304. *A Conclusion.* It is almost a year since I first thought of writing this book. I was recently told that my students are preparing a tribute to me on my seventy-sixth birthday.

Before falling asleep I thought once more of that banquet in my honor last year, but the memory was quickly displaced by the image of a medieval mitred abbot or saint. I must have seen that statue. Where was it? Perhaps on the old Spreuer bridge in Lucerne. Is there not also the *Danse des Morts* in the Musée d'Art? Was it there?

In any event, the two lines below the priest's picture re-emerge:

> *Nun bin ich alt, an Ehren reich*
> *Jetzt kommt der Tod sogleich.*
>
> [I am now old, many honors conferred on me
> Now I must face death immediately.]

305. Diogenes returning: A Greek patient had an amusing fantasy: The famous Cynic philosopher Diogenes of Sinope lands, more than two thousand years after his death, in New York. He wanders into the Stock Exchange and seeks all around Broad and Wall streets for an honest man. He finally shrugs his shoulders and, irrevocably resigned, blows out his lantern, wearied from the vain search.

306. *In Retrospect:* When one as an old man looks back on oneself as a lad and even in the years of manhood (as Max Beerbohm's contrasting the old with the young self) one will recognize a particular characteristic of youth. How rigidly moralistic and cruelly intolerant one was in one's opinion about others and even about oneself! One

almost thought people should have no moral failings and weaknesses, no malice or cruel tendencies, no crude sexual desires that conflicted with their life as members of the family. And the worst of it was not that one had those prejudices, but one also proclaimed them and acted on them, looked down on others and often on oneself—and unhesitatingly condemned them. We lacked gentle tolerance and benevolence toward human nature and we did not acknowledge its narrow limitations.

307. *Last Day of 1963:* After he had examined me and written his prescriptions, Dr. Alfred Vogl, my physician for many years, and I chatted. He smiled when he heard the story of Gutel Rothschild, the first lady of the Frankfurt banking house. Her physician had regretfully told her "Alas, I cannot make you younger." The aged woman answered: "I don't expect that, Doctor. I want only to become older." During our conversation I had also mentioned that a new book of mine would be published in 1964.

We shook hands. Leaving the excellent internist who had enabled me to keep on writing, I wished him a happy New Year. Instead of wishing me many more years, he said in a graceful variation: "I wish you to write many more good books."

A conclusion

When one has reached one's seventy-sixth year one's thoughts are rarely any longer directed to the future and are frequently occupied with memories. A recently published book brought a new reminiscence of Freud to the surface.* Accident was responsible that the Swiss pastor Oskar Pfister and I once met in the waiting room of Freud, with whom he had an appointment. We already knew each other and talked. Freud had a visitor who, it seemed, did not want to leave. We heard later it was the professor of psychiatry Gustav Aschaffenburg, whom Freud considered a bore. Freud opened the door and came out for a minute. Turning to Pfister and alluding to the tedious visitor, Freud asked: "Tell me, is it valid that religion still forbids us to kill people even in one's thoughts?"

The memory that is for me personally more important will be found in a letter Freud wrote Pfister, dated December 21, 1924.† Pastor Pfister had made, it seemed, the acquaintance of a young neurotic American. Freud tells Pfister he need not worry about the young man who could be helped and continues: "Dr. Reik here in Vienna has specialized in these severe obsessional neuroses, he treated

---

* Sigmund Freud, *Psychoanalysis and Faith,* Dialogues with the Reverend Oskar Pfister. Edited by Heinrich Meng and Ernst L. Freud.
† P. 96 of the quoted book.

a Russian count whom I sent him, for instance, with extreme patience and deep understanding and not without success for several years."

The case of the Russian count and of his severe neurosis were presented in my book *Dogma and Compulsion*. What delights me in Freud's letter is that he had—even forty years ago—such trust in my psychoanalytic talent. What now saddens me a little is that I did not fulfill all his expectations. Now it's too late for that and I am humming a song of my contemporary Maurice Chevalier, *"On est comme on est,"* wherewith this book is brought to a resigned and serene conclusion.